Solution
Focused
Coaching

First published in Great Britain in 2001 by
Go MAD Books
Pocket Gate Farm
Off Breakback Road
Woodhouse Eaves
Leicestershire
LE12 8RS

ISBN 978-0-9933414-1-0
British Library Cataloguing in Publication Data.

**ThinkOn® is a registered trademark and trading name of
Go M.A.D. Ltd**

This book was originally published with the title 'Go MAD About Coaching.'

This book is dedicated to people who seek to help others be successful; to those solution focused thinkers who have not yet experienced the personal satisfaction of coaching someone else to make a difference; and to all who aspire to be great coaches.

"If there were ever a time to dare,
to make a difference,
to embark on something worth doing,
it is now.
Not for any grand cause, necessarily –
but for something that tugs at your heart,
something that's your aspiration,
something that's your dream.

You owe it to yourself
to make your days here count.
Have fun.
Dig deep.
Stretch.
Dream big."

(from an Apple Macintosh computer ad, 1991)

And, of course, to everyone who recognises the importance of continuing to learn and develop their ability to make a difference.

Andy Gilbert,
Developer of the ThinkOn® Results Framework

Contents	Page

ABOUT THE AUTHORS — 9

INTRODUCTION

1. Who is this book for? — 11
2. Getting the most from this book — 12
3. Read with a purpose — 14
4. Coaching, mentoring, counselling – what's the difference? — 15
5. A word of warning — 16

PART ONE: LET'S GET STARTED - UNDERSTANDING THINKON®

6. ThinkOn® – the background research — 19
7. The ThinkOn® Key Principles — 20
8. The ThinkOn® approach to coaching — 22
9. What makes a great ThinkOn® coach? — 23
10. The ThinkOn® Results Framework — 25
11. SITBACC – 11 critical links — 28
12. ThinkOn® – a multi-purpose tool — 41
13. 26 areas of personal competence — 42
14. Working the triangles — 44
15. A pause to reflect on learning so far — 45

PART TWO: LINKING THINKON® WITH HIGH QUALITY QUESTIONS

16. The answers are on the inside — 47
17. What is a high quality question? — 48
18. Essential stuff to know about the different types of questions — 51
19. Two types of high quality question — 54
20. Every question has a purpose — 56
21. Control the system, not the content — 57
22. Content free coaching — 57
23. A 40 question coaching script — 58
24. The sound of silence — 62
25. Being creative with H.Q.Q.'s — 62
26. Case study example — 63
27. A blank page — 69
28. The classic ThinkOn® coaching route — 70
29. Using alternative routes — 75
30. A shorter "blind" coaching script — 76
31. A pause to reflect on learning so far — 79

PART THREE: THE THINKON® SYSTEM IN GREATER DETAIL

Section One

32. Identifying the strength of reason why – key points   81
33. High quality questions to ask   82
34. Linking the reason why with other ThinkOn® Key Principles   84
35. What to watch out for: reason why   85

Section Two

36. The importance of defining the goal   88
37. Defining the goal – key points   88
38. Differentiating between umbrella goals and SMART goals   90
39. Case study example – umbrella goal   91
40. Defining SMART goals   97
41. Defining measurable qualitative goals   99
42. Case study example – qualitative goal   100
43. Visioning - using imagination to define sensory specific goals   106
44. High quality questions to ask   108
45. Linking the defined goal with other ThinkOn® Key Principles   111
46. What to watch out for: defining goals   113

Section Three

47. Generating possibilities – 10 common areas   115
48. High quality questions to ask   118
49. Effective phrasing of possibility questions   120
50. Possible reasons to involve others   122
51. Think laterally about who to involve   123
52. Gaining buy-in from others   125
53. Possible ways to help others generate possibilities   126
54. What to watch out for when generating possibilities   127
55. More tips and techniques that work   130
56. A pause to reflect on learning so far   132

Section Four

57. Deciding priorities   133
58. High quality questions to ask   134
59. Defining SMART sub-goals   136

Section Five

60. Building confidence – key points   137
61. Linking self-belief with the other ThinkOn® Key Principles   140
62. High quality questions to ask   142
63. What to watch out for: self-belief   143
64. Ways to maintain or increase self-belief   145

Section Six

65. Planning in time to take action   147

Section Seven

66.	Testing commitment and personal responsibility	149
67.	High quality questions to ask	149
68.	Linking personal responsibility with the other ThinkOn® Key Principles	150
69.	What to watch out for: personal responsibility	152
70.	A couple of tips	153
71.	The final questions – celebrating success	153

Section Eight

72.	Agreeing the way forward	154
73.	Reviewing progress	155
74.	A pause to reflect on learning so far	155

PART FOUR: TIPS, TECHNIQUES AND SITUATIONS

75.	More tips about coaching	157
76.	Self-coaching tips	159
77.	Coaching the opposite sex	159
78.	Developing a state of relaxed concentration	159
79.	Useful knowledge (coaching made more complex!)	160
80.	Increasing awareness	160
81.	Offering feedback	161
82.	Giving advice and information	162
83.	Coaching during organisational change and restructuring	162
84.	Coaching people you love	164
85.	A few other uses for high quality questions	165
86.	Coaching upwards	166
87.	Answering a question with a question	167
88.	Listening skills	168
89.	When coaching doesn't work	171
90.	ThinkOn® as a 20 step self-coaching process	171
91.	Practise, practise, practise	173
92.	Leave the how for later	174

SUCCESS STORIES, CASE STUDIES AND FURTHER INFORMATION

93.	Mike's story – career success	175
94.	Anna's story – business success	177
95.	Tracey's story – sporting success	177
96.	Natalie's story – child success	179
97.	Kraft Foods – financial success	180
98.	John's poem – personal success	183
99.	Applying the ThinkOn® System at four levels	184
100.	Leadership thinking and cultural transformation	184
101.	ThinkOn® information and resources	187

"I like things to happen; and if they don't happen,
I like to make them happen."
Winston Churchill

ABOUT THE AUTHORS

Andy Gilbert is the developer of the critically acclaimed ThinkOn® Results Framework. As Managing Director of Go M.A.D. Thinking, he is passionate about helping people Go Make A Difference by developing their thinking in a solution focused way.

Andy is the author of over 20 books, videos and audio programmes including The Art of Making A Difference and How to Save Time & Money by Managing Organisational Change Effectively. His podcast series 'Thinking For Business Success' has regularly been at the top of the iTunes Business podcast chart and has been downloaded by over two million people.

Andy has gathered a wealth of knowledge and experience as a top-level executive coach and business improvement expert working with leaders in over 250 organisations. He is also constantly exploring ways of using new media and technology to allow the world to access great thinking and coaching tools in line with his 2028 vision of being a catalyst for 1000 humanitarian projects.

Ian Chakravorty started his management career in the glass industry before fulfilling his deeply held desire to become a maths teacher. During a successful teaching career, he took a 12-month sabbatical to work with Andy and undertake the original research that led to the development of the ThinkOn® Results Framework. He never returned to full-time teaching, choosing instead to continue the research and applications of the Results Framework to help individuals and organisations achieve greater results.

"Whatever we do for someone else we do
because it fulfils a need we have."
M. Scott Peck

INTRODUCTION

1. Who is this book for?

Hello ... And welcome to Solution Focused Thinking.

There is a high probability that you are reading this book for one of two reasons. The obvious one is that you want to develop your coaching skills to help others. Alternatively your reason might be to help yourself. Either is fine!

Our purpose in writing this book is threefold:

- To help managers and leaders develop the ability of others in their team to individually and collectively make a difference that ultimately contributes to the success of the organisation.

- To help individuals use a solution focused thinking system to help themselves and others.

- To make coaching easy to understand and apply.

Having developed the ThinkOn® Results Framework and applied it worldwide to accelerate results and enable change, I know that it can help you achieve greater success – dependent upon your answer to one critical question:

How serious are you about making a difference?

Coaching is just one application of the ThinkOn® Results Framework. Whilst you will find it useful to read the original book, "The Art of Making A Difference" for your own development, this book does not require any prior ThinkOn® knowledge or experience. It has been written for pragmatists and results orientated people. The content is deliberately low on theory and high on practical tips, ideas and questions designed to make people think. We do not waste time aiming to convince you of the benefits of coaching, let's just agree that it is an important part of a manager's role to develop people's ability to think in a solution focused way. Our definition of coaching is very simple: it's just one person helping another person to think and move forwards by asking high quality questions.

However, before you dive into the book it is appropriate to issue a few words of warning! You will not become a great coach by just reading this book - only by applying what you have learned and practising your skills. Understanding the process and skills of coaching needs to be balanced with understanding people and this can most easily be done by working with them in a coaching role. In other words you don't become a great coach by doing it by the book!

2. Getting the most from this book

Allow me to explain how the book is structured and then I will give you several helpful ideas about how to get the most out of it.

There are four main parts to this book:

Part One provides an understanding of the background research, the seven ThinkOn® Key Principles. the ThinkOn® Results Framework and what makes a great ThinkOn® coach.

Part Two focuses on the development and use of high quality coaching questions. It provides examples of how to structure sessions using the ThinkOn® Results Framework.

Part Three is divided into eight sections, each one focusing on a different aspect of a ThinkOn® coaching session. Each of the sections contains chapters which cover: the main learning points relating to each key success principle; a reminder of how that key principle links with other key principles; examples of high quality questions; how to decide what to do next; tips and tools that have been proven to work; things to watch out for; and finally, an opportunity to reflect on what you have gained from that section.

Part Four contains a collection of tips and techniques together with guidance on a variety of coaching situations and applications (useful stuff that is not specific to ThinkOn® coaching).

The final section contains a selection of success stories and case studies. These illustrate the flexibility of using ThinkOn® as a thinking system to get results.

This book does not pretend to be the definitive, or the most comprehensive, guide to coaching. It is more about how to help others make a difference. Once you are familiar with the ThinkOn® Results Framework, which will be explained shortly, you will easily be able to follow the structure of the book. This means that you will quickly gain access to ideas, tips and examples relevant to each stage of the coaching session.

The chapters are deliberately short so that you can always finish reading to the end of a chapter in less than a couple of minutes! We have also included several of our favourite quotes throughout the book. Each is relevant to the theme of that particular part of the book and is provided for inspiration or reflection. For example:

> **"Any fact facing us is not as important as our attitude toward it, for that determines our success or failure."**
> **Norman Vincent Peale**

If this is your personal copy of the book, I encourage you to write in it. The questions and exercises included are there for a purpose and the margins are deliberately wide to provide space for making notes. I mention this because in " The Art of Making A Difference," I emphasised the same point and evidence has shown that the people who wrote in the book gained significantly greater benefit than those who just read it. In fact my favourite response to people who tell me how much they like one of my books is to ask them the question, "Did you write in it?" Of course it depends upon your answer to the question I asked you earlier, i.e.

How serious are you about making a difference?

Now, I hope you don't mind me challenging you like this. It's just that I've discovered over the years that this is a useful question to ask. You will notice throughout this book that I ask questions designed to make you think, and I encourage you to answer these questions as you read.

3. Read with a purpose

As you read, focus on the reason why you are reading this book. What is the difference you want to make? Who will benefit from your development? Keep this purpose at the forefront of your mind to help you identify the most useful content. When you re-read this book, or parts of it, you will notice things that take on a new relevance as your purpose or situation changes. The most obvious difference is whether you are reading this to coach others or to develop your ability to coach yourself. It doesn't matter which, as both the ThinkOn® system and coaching skills are transferable to any situation.

There are several self-coaching exercises contained within this book. Before you get to them, you will need to focus on a difference you want to make. It can be a large or small difference – work or non-work related – either is fine.

Make a note of your desired difference below:

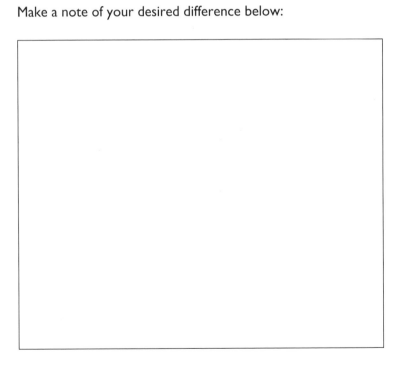

Yes, of course, I'm testing you. Are you serious about making a difference? Have you written anything? Go on, I dare you –nobody will read it – you can always change your mind later. Just because you write something doesn't mean it is set in concrete!

4. Coaching, mentoring, counselling – what's the difference?

For various reasons, many people like to have definitions of what coaching is and isn't. However, it is useful to remember that a definition is only the viewpoint of another person. I have found that it is often more helpful to develop an understanding and personal viewpoint about the differences between coaching, mentoring and counselling.

Perhaps the easiest place to start is with counselling, which focuses on helping people deal with problems they have or are experiencing. In most counselling processes there is a significant emphasis on the past, as this is where the problem exists or originated. However, with coaching the emphasis is on future success and being proactive to opportunities. In other words, you don't need a problem to be coached! Successful, high performing people from all professions are increasingly turning towards coaching as a means to helping them be even more successful.

> "The measure of success is not whether you have a tough problem to deal with, but whether it's the same problem as you had last year."
> John Foster Dulles

So what about mentoring? Well, this term originated in Homer's Odyssey when Odysseus, the King of Ithaca, went travelling and left his son, Telemachus, in the capable hands of Mentor. Telemachus was very young when his father left, so Mentor was carefully selected as he was a wise and proven teacher – which was a good thing to do as Odysseus didn't return for 21 years! During this time, Mentor passed on his knowledge and skills, and he encouraged Telemachus to develop as a whole person.

Nowadays, mentoring usually means establishing a longer-term relationship between an individual and a more experienced mentor. It typically covers a broader range of issues than counselling or coaching. Mentoring can involve advising, teaching and counselling another person to gain skills and experience in order to develop their career.

Coaching is not teaching. It is about helping people to think in a helpful, solution focused way that improves personal or team performance. However, it requires no technical expertise or familiarity with the subject matter. Coaching is a process and skillset that facilitates change and development; it is about helping individuals and teams invent the future and take steps towards achieving it.

> "Building awareness and responsibility is the
> essence of good coaching."
> John Whitmore

5. A word of warning

Part One of this book is designed to help you understand the ThinkOn® Results Framework. It comprises 29 pages contained within 10 important chapters. Reading this information for the first time might cause you to feel an overwhelming sense of, "Wow – will I ever be able to apply various principles, remember lots of questions and understand the ThinkOn® Results Framework?"

The answer is "Yes. However, be patient!" Developing coaching skills and expertise takes time and is a gradual process. The following points show the sequence of learning that has proved most effective in helping people to develop as great ThinkOn® coaches:

1. Understand the ThinkOn® Results Framework.

2. Understand more about coaching.

3. Understand how to apply ThinkOn® to coaching.

4. Understand and practise the use of high quality questions.

5. Refine your use of ThinkOn® as a coaching methodology.

6. Use the ThinkOn® Results Framework and build onto it additional skills and techniques.

7. Practise, practise, practise until competent.

"You cannot expect to arrive at full competence,
without making a start and
learning along the way."
Ian Chakravorty

As you progress through this book, keep in mind that the best is yet to come!

"Any intelligent fool can make things bigger
and more complex...
It takes a touch of genius and a lot of courage
to move in the opposite direction."
E. F. Schumacher

PART ONE: LET'S GET STARTED – UNDERSTANDING THINKON®

6. THINKON® – the background research

You have made thousands of differences in your life and continue to make differences each and every day. However, most people are unaware of what they naturally do whenever they achieve success in life. So back in 1998, we decided to take on the mammoth task of discovering exactly what it was that people did when they were successful at making a difference. And we wanted to know for a really good reason. If we could map out the success principles that people naturally used we could share that with everyone and we would all be able to increase the probability of turning our dreams into reality, no matter how big or small.

So we got busy. We interviewed all kinds of people making all kinds of differences; from doubling the sales turnover of large corporate organisations and increasing production by 100% to changing career later in life and running a marathon. We dug deep and looked far and wide and, over 4,000 hours of research later, we identified that people were naturally applying seven key success principles to go make a difference (or Go M.A.D. as we originally referred to it) and these linked to form a results framework. We soon realised that the widest possible application for this framework is to help people think in a solution focused way in order to solve problems and achieve their goals.

Fast forward to today and the original framework with its seven key principles is as relevant today as it ever was. Now the ThinkOn® Results Framework is used in over 40 countries across the world and has helped organisations, teams and individuals achieve incredible results in business transformation and improvement, sporting performance, health and fitness, education, financial security and career development. You name it, it's been used to make it happen! Of course the world has been changing at an ever-increasing pace and so have we. Our original framework has now developed into a complete thinking system that's intuitive to use and easy to understand. We've added tools and techniques to enable change and accelerate results, joined the digital revolution and even more passionate people have joined our team. And as we've grown and developed over the past twenty years, so have the many uses and applications of the ThinkOn® Results Framework with coaching being one of the most powerful applications to help yourself and to help others. But one thing remains constant in all of this change; our relentless passion for helping others to make the differences they want to make.

So, if you're interested about helping people with their thinking, let's get stuck in!

Andy Gilbert
Managing Director
ThinkOn®

7. The ThinkOn® Key Principles

The following seven key principles are the basic components of your natural framework for being successful:

1. **Having a strong reason why** – it takes a strong reason why to maintain motivation and commitment.

2. **Defining your goal** – be clear on what you want to achieve, so you can measure your success.

3. **Exploring Possibilities and Planning Priorities** – having completed the why and the what, this principle moves you onto the how. Generate ideas, consider possibilities, prioritise and plan in the time to achieve your goal.

4. **Having self-belief** – have you got what it takes? The knowledge, skills, resources and confidence. Develop the self-belief that you can make a difference.

5. **Involving others** – you will achieve the greatest results by working with others and obtaining their buy-in.

6. **Taking personal responsibility** – be accountable, a role model to others and make your own choices.

7. **Taking action and measuring the results.**

Principle One considers WHY you want to make a difference.

Principle Two focuses on WHAT difference you want to make.

Principles Three – Seven concentrate on HOW to make the difference.

Many people have commented to me, "Andy, this is common sense." And, of course, it is! It is also day-to-day common practice for the hundreds of small differences we make. Let me give you an example of how you have applied these principles to make a difference in the past 24 hours.

1. "I'm getting hungry." = Strong reason why to make a difference.

2. "I'm going to get something to eat within the next 30 minutes." = Defined goal.

3. "Should I buy some food or prepare a meal?" = Possibilities and priorities.

4. "I've got sufficient time and money." = Self-belief.

5. "Who will prepare or buy my food?" = Involve others.

6. "It's down to me to decide and make time to eat." = Personal responsibility.

7. "Meal over and I am no longer hungry." = Action taken and results measured.

If everyone uses these key principles naturally, what is the point of ThinkOn® and this book? Well, hopefully the answer is obvious. If not, here are several thoughts to consider:

People do not apply this thinking consistently – especially at work.

People are largely unaware of this natural thinking for the small differences they repetitiously make.

People can be helped to become consciously aware of what is helping/hindering their success.

"The role of a ThinkOn® coach is to help others develop their thinking and hence their ability to make a difference."
Andy Gilbert

---

8. The ThinkOn® approach to coaching

There are several good coaching models, and you might already be familiar with, or use, a particular one. Before I discovered ThinkOn® and applied it in a coaching context, my particular favourites were the GROW and Inner Game coaching models, which I used to develop my coaching skills. However, having discovered how the ThinkOn® Key Principles linked together, it became easier to use a more structured coaching method that was based entirely upon natural success principles.

The ThinkOn® approach places the emphasis on achieving results through keeping the coaching method as simple as possible and adopting a structured solution focus.

The coach uses the ThinkOn® Results Framework to structure high quality questions designed to help the individual think about why, what and how to make a difference. Through the use of these questions, the coach encourages the individual to consciously apply the key success principles contained within the ThinkOn® Results Framework.

The core ThinkOn® coaching skill is the use of high quality questions. Listening and observation skills are also important, but it is possible to coach, using the ThinkOn® system, without hearing or seeing the responses to your questions. Hence ThinkOn® coaching deliberately adopts a detached approach to the content of the coaching session, by focusing on the components of the system which will help the individual with their thinking. In simple terms, the coach is a systems thinker who avoids getting sucked into the coaching content or subject matter. Whereas the person seeking to make a difference is encouraged to take responsibility for understanding their circumstances and deciding how to make a difference.

"Give help rather than advice."
Luc de Clapiers

The greatest help a coach can be is to guide an individual through the framework of making a difference and help that person take personal responsibility for being successful.

9. What makes a great ThinkOn® Coach?

Listed below are thirty of my beliefs about qualities and attributes that contribute to becoming a great coach.

– The ability to suspend your own agenda and judgement about the difference that others are seeking to make.

– Focusing on helping the individual build awareness of themselves and their environment.

– Developing and asking high quality questions.

– The awareness to differentiate between coaching method and content.

– A passion for helping others make a difference.

– Resisting the urge to problem solve, provide expertise or give answers.

- A belief that individuals can achieve more.

- Being able to relax and work with anyone seeking to make a difference.

- Being supportive, yet challenging.

- Using a range of flexible and creative techniques to generate possibilities.

- Allowing the individual to do the thinking and exploring in their mind.

- Recognising that the responsibility for making a difference lies with the individual.

- Practising skills to engage the imagination.

- Understanding that different people see the same thing in different ways (their map of reality) and have different reasons for wanting, or doing, things.

- Remaining ego-less when coaching.

- Having a high self-awareness of your thoughts/feelings/values and recognising these will not only differ from those of the individual being coached, but might also get in the way of helping that person to make a difference.

- Continuing to learn and apply that learning.

- Distinguishing between trivial and significant issues.

- The ability to identify self-limiting or enabling beliefs of the individual or team being coached.

- Providing accurate feedback in specific behavioural terms.

- Building a relationship of trust and understanding without dependency.

- Maintaining high levels of personal self-confidence and self-esteem.

- Having your heart in the right place.

"Life's most persistent and urgent question is:
What are you doing for others?"
Martin Luther King Jr.

– Observing all that is happening and giving attention to that which is not happening.

– Having a positive expectation of people's potential.

– Keeping the emphasis of the coaching focused on the future.

– Phrasing language in present and future tense.

– Role modelling personal use of ThinkOn®.

– Developing a state of relaxed concentration by paying total attention to the individual, without concentrating on techniques.

– Having fun and celebrating success.

At this point I realise the list might appear a little daunting and you might not fully understand some of these attributes. However, continue to read and your understanding will develop. The following two chapters illustrate the ThinkOn® Results Framework and explain some easy ways of remembering it.

10. The ThinkOn® Results Framework

The following diagram provides a useful framework to consciously apply the key principles and start to understand the links between them.

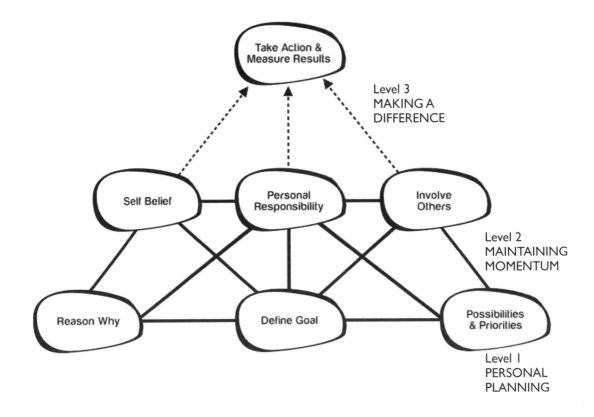

ThinkOn® Results Framework

Notice the three levels of the pyramid. The first level I refer to as *personal planning* and it links principles one, two and three. These are the foundations upon which success is built. It takes a *strong reason why* (principle one) to maintain motivation, face challenges and overcome obstacles. Hence, this is a cornerstone. The other cornerstone is provided by a well-constructed *plan of priorities* (principle three) underpinned by some robust possibility thinking. These principles are linked by having a *defined goal* (principle two) to centrally support the remaining four principles.

Priorities cannot be planned without a defined goal, and the goal cannot be achieved without a strong enough reason to make a difference. With these foundations in place, a second level can be built.

The second level I refer to as **maintaining momentum** and this builds upon the personal planning of the foundation level. Having the **self-belief** (principle four) to succeed in making a difference is dependent upon having a defined goal which, you believe, is possible to achieve. Without the self-belief and the desire to achieve, progress will falter. Hence, the link between principles one and four.

Involving others (principle five) should be built into the plan and prioritised. However, to do it successfully takes both skill and effort in order to continue moving in the right direction. The defined goal and plan of priorities established at the foundation level will need to be communicated and both might need to be revised following the involvement of others. Without this involvement, and the additional support it brings, it might be impossible to move to the next level.

At the centre of the framework is the choice every individual has of taking **personal responsibility** for their actions (principle six) to make a difference. If this choice is exercised then the other key principles, with which it links, stand a chance of being applied. However, in order to move to the third level all of the first six principles have to be in place.

The third level is that of **making a difference** and can only be reached by building the foundations with the first three principles and maintaining the momentum by applying principles four, five and six. Even then, it is still necessary to **take action and measure the results** (principle seven) to know that the goal has been achieved and a difference has been made.

"To accomplish great things, we must not only
act, but also dream; not only plan, but also
believe."
Anatole France

11. SITBACC – 11 critical links

To effectively use the ThinkOn® Results Framework as a coach,
it is important to understand in more detail the eleven critical
links between the first six key principles. The mnemonic
SITBACC is a useful reminder of these. Starting at the reason
why, follow the arrows between the first five key principles to
spell SITBAC. The final C of this mnemonic represents the five
choice lines that link personal responsibility to the other key
principles.

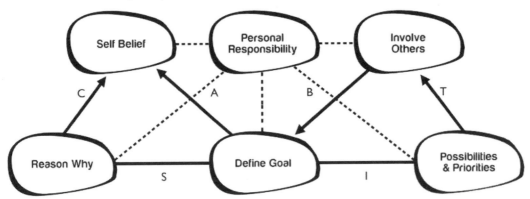

Strength

Importance

Task

Buy-in

Achievability

Check

Choices x5 (indicated by dotted lines)

28

The link between the first and second key principle is known as the *Strength* line.

To make a difference, the reason for making that difference has to be sufficiently strong. It is not good enough to have a reason and simply know what it is; it has to be powerful enough to survive any potential setbacks. A goal without a strong reason why will not be pursued in times of difficulty.

"**You can measure the strength of a desire by the obstacles it is capable of overcoming.**"
W. Timothy Gallwey

The link between the second and third key principle is referred to as the *Importance* line.

Possibilities & Priorities is a three-stage process of generating possibilities, prioritising those possibilities and planning in time to do the important ones. In order to prioritise it is necessary to refer back to the defined goal to determine which possibility is most important. Hence the link.

The link between the third and fifth key principle is referred to as the *Task* line.

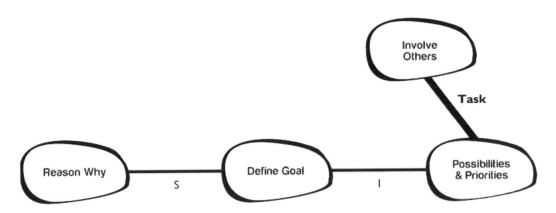

The first stage of the planning priorities process involves generating and exploring possibilities & priorities about several things. These include possible tasks to undertake, possible people to involve and possible ways in which they could help, as well as identifying possible obstacles and ways of overcoming them.

"The future belongs to people who see possibilities before they become obvious."
Theodore Levitt

The link between the second and fifth key principle is referred to as the *Buy-in* line.

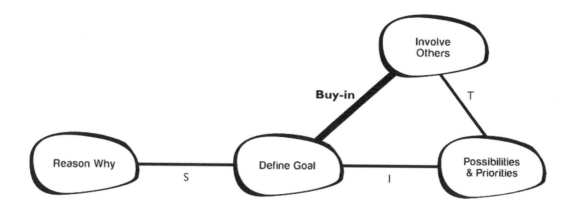

To get others involved in helping to achieve your goal you will first need to get them to buy-in to it being worthwhile. Notice, in the ThinkOn® Results Framework, that there is no direct link between your reason why (principle one) and involving others (principle five). The conduit is via the defined goal. In other words, you need to be able to communicate to others not just what you want to achieve, but also why that difference is important to you. Hence the Buy-in line refers to the use of communication and influencing skills. In order to obtain this buy-in from others it might be necessary, on occasions, to redefine your goal in order to make it more acceptable to them and obtain essential support.

"Our best thoughts come from others."
Ralph Waldo Emerson

The link between the second and fourth key principle is known as the *Achievability* line.

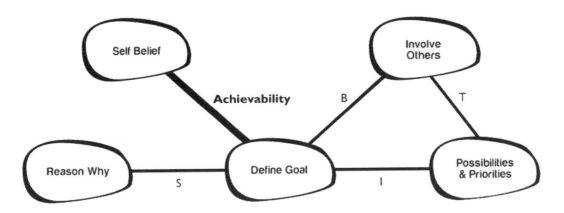

This is an assessment of how achievable you believe your goal to be, i.e. to what extent do you believe you have got what it takes in order to achieve the difference? In order to answer this question, it is necessary to consider the timescale of the goal and level of achievement that has been defined, together with your level of skill, knowledge, available resources and confidence.

"If I have the belief that I can do it, I shall surely acquire the capacity to do it even if I may not have it at the beginning."

Mahatma Gandhi

The link between the first and fourth key principle is referred to as the *Check* line.

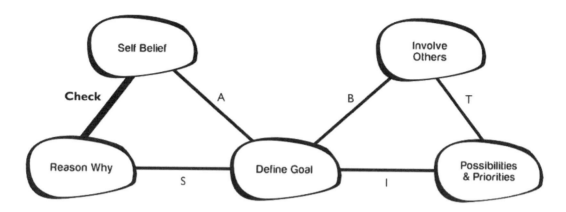

It is common during coaching sessions for an individual's level of self- belief to change or fluctuate. Often it will increase as the ThinkOn® coaching reveals how that person can achieve the difference they want to make. Likewise, the strength of reason why can alter.

Occasionally it might fall if the prioritised plan is likely to involve too much effort. In order to make a difference an individual needs to maintain high levels of both self-belief and reason why. One without the other will not suffice. Hence, the need to check these levels at various stages when coaching.

"Doubt is the vestibule through which all must pass before they can enter into the temple of wisdom."

Charles Caleb Colton

The sixth key principle is linked to the first five key principles by separate *Choice* lines.

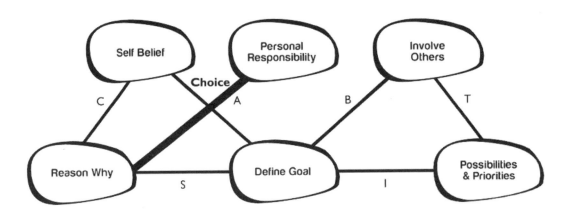

You have to take personal responsibility for choosing whether or not to think about your level of motivation and reasons for wanting to make a difference. Can you be bothered? If so, how strongly?

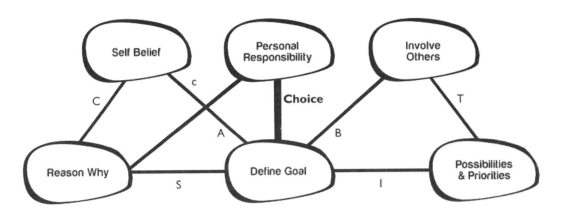

You have to choose how well defined your goal is. Will you take personal responsibility for turning a vague aim or wish into a specific, measurable, time-dated goal? It's your choice.

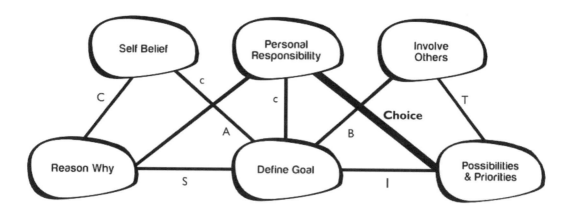

You also have to take personal responsibility for generating possibilities and deciding exactly how much time you will spend on each priority. How much time have you chosen to set aside in your diary?

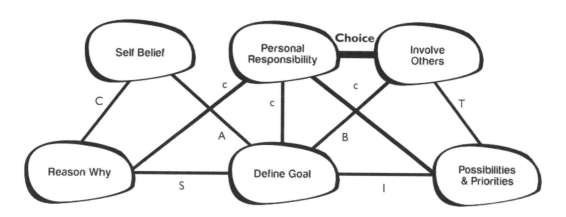

You decide who to involve; what to involve others in; how, when and where to involve others; and how to obtain their buy-in. There are many choices to be made if you are prepared to take personal responsibility for making a difference.

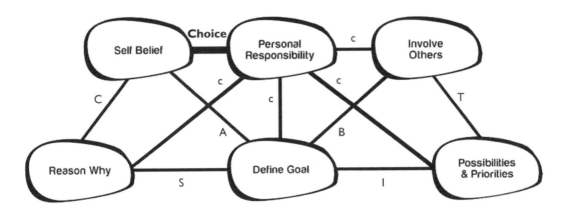

I often refer to this link as the choice we have to make about taking responsibility for our own development. This final choice line links principles four and six together. Are you prepared to assess your capabilities, confidence, knowledge, skills and experience and to ask yourself the question, "Have I got what it takes?"

If the answer is "No", are you prepared to take personal responsibility for developing yourself?

So there you have it – the first six key principles and the eleven critical links between them – seventeen elements of the ThinkOn® Results Framework. Before you read any further, it is important to consolidate your understanding and assess your learning so far.

TIME TO WRITE

An exercise that participants on our coaching development programmes find particularly useful is to practise drawing the framework and labelling the various links. Doing this several times will help to imprint the key elements of the coaching in your memory. It also helps to draw the framework and explain it to another person.

To make it easy for you, I have given you a helping hand on the following page. So pick up your pen and practise.

Remember to draw and label the link lines.

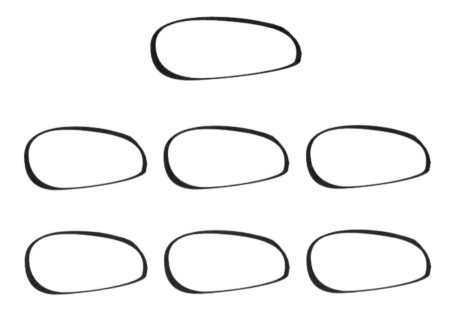

S _ _ _ _ _ _ _

I _ _ _ _ _ _ _ _ _

T _ _ _

B _ _ _ _

A _ _ _ _ _ _ _ _ _ _ _ _ _

C _ _ _ _

C _ _ _ _ _ _

TIME TO REFLECT

Think about a time in your life when you set out to make a difference and were successful in achieving it. It can be a small or large, personal or work-related difference. Now, with this in mind, reflect on the ThinkOn® Results Framework and answer the following 16 questions:

Principle One:	–	**What was the reason for wanting to make a difference?**
	–	**How strong was my reason?**
Principle Two	–	**What specifically did I want to achieve?**
	–	**How did I intend to measure my success?**
Principle Three	–	**What were some of the possibilities I considered? (tasks, involvement of others, implications, challenges to be faced)**
	–	**What were my most important priorities?**
Principle Four	–	**How high was my self-belief that I had what it took to be successful?**

                  –   **What sort of messages (helpful thoughts) was I giving myself?**

                  –   **What did I do to maintain/increase my confidence?**

Principle Five: –   **Who did I involve to help me?**

                  –   **How did I gain their buy-in?**

Principle Six   –   **What did I take personal responsibility for doing?**

                  –   **How much time did I set aside to do these important priorities?**

                  –   **What critical decisions and choices did I make?**

Principle Seven: –   **What action did I take?**

                  –   **How did I measure the results of success?**

What have you discovered or realised? Probably that you have already successfully used the ThinkOn® Key Principles without realising it!

Now it's time to consider the flipside. This time think of a time in the past when you set out to make a difference but, for whatever reason, you were unsuccessful. Refer to the ThinkOn® Results Framework and use it as a diagnostic tool to identify the causes.

Which key principles were not applied or could have been applied more effectively?

Which links in the framework were either weak or missing?

What have you noticed? If you consider another couple of personal examples can you identify any common patterns? It is usual that most people will be naturally stronger at applying some parts of the ThinkOn® Results Framework than other parts.

12. ThinkOn® – a multi purpose tool

The last exercises focused on using ThinkOn® as a way of challenging and learning from past experience, whereas the rest of this book focuses on the use of ThinkOn® as a development framework to help others be successful in the *future*. Remember, of course, that ThinkOn® can easily be used as an analysis tool to assess *current* progress on differences that are being made.

> *"Anyone can increase their probability of success through the conscious application of natural success principles. Learning how to do this is easy; doing it consistently takes time and effort."*
> **Ian Chakravorty**

When using ThinkOn® as a solution focused thinking system it is important to build your existing knowledge and skills onto the Results Framework. Recognise that ThinkOn® does not replace or supersede anything that currently exists; it is simply a well-researched, flexible tool that can sit alongside the rest of your tools, techniques and expertise, or underpin them as a framework for success.

13. 26 areas of personal competence

By now, I trust you have realised that the ThinkOn® Results Framework encompasses a wide variety of skill and knowledge areas that can be studied and developed independently of each other. These can be combined to form personal or organisational development plans and programmes, together with assessment tools, designed to increase and measure people's ability to make a measurable difference. Listed below are 26 development areas:

– self-motivation	– leadership
– goal defining (SMART)	– mental programming
– vision and values alignment	– self-awareness
– use of imagination	– confidence building
– possibility based thinking	– team working and delegation
– idea generation	– relationship building
– risk assessment	– communication
– problem solving	– influencing
– prioritising	– decision making
– project planning	– taking responsibility
– time/self-management	– role modelling
– resource analysis	– taking action
– personal development planning (P.D.P.)	– results monitoring

> "If you want 1 year of prosperity, grow grain.
> If you want 10 years of prosperity, grow trees.
> If you want 100 years of prosperity, grow people."
> **Chinese proverb**

The following diagram illustrates the relationship of these development areas within the framework. It is important for a coach to recognise that the individual being coached might need help or development in one or more of these areas in order to achieve their goal.

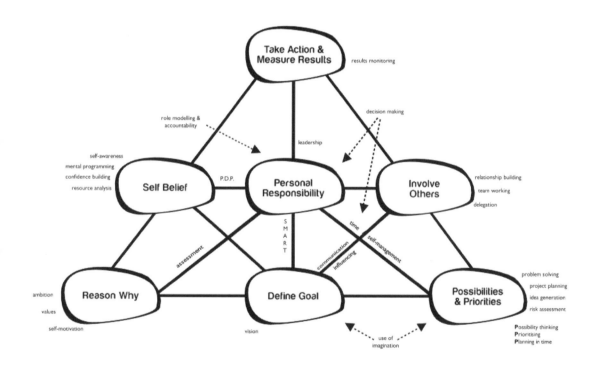

14. Working the triangles

When I am training others to coach using the ThinkOn®
Framework, I often find myself encouraging them to "work the
triangles." This is perhaps easiest to illustrate by splitting the
framework into two. One triangle focuses attention on the
"softer internal" issues and encompasses motivation, confidence,
values, feelings, aspirations and vision. In other words, the stuff
that is normally hidden from others and kept to ourself. The
second triangle relates to the more tangible factors that are
easier to see, touch and have "external hard" evidence of.

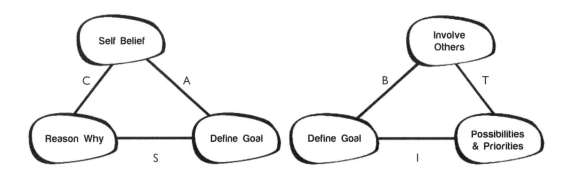

Internal (softer issues)
Motivation, values, feelings,
confidence, self image, aspirations,
vision, self awareness.

external (harder issues)
Objectives, ideas tasks, priorities,
actions, plans, timescales, logistics,
people.

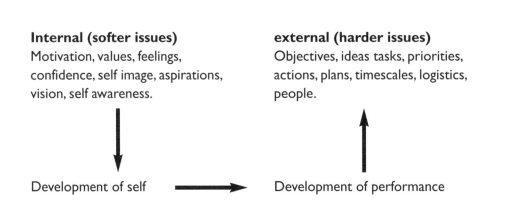

Development of self   ➜   Development of performance

When coaching others to make a difference it is important to ensure that the first triangle is strong enough to support the rest of the ThinkOn® Results Framework. There is no point in moving on to asking high quality questions about possibilities and planning priorities, if the individual lacks confidence or the goal conflicts with their personal values.

15. A pause to reflect on learning so far

I have deliberately taken a very logical and structured approach to explaining ThinkOn®. I am also aware that you might be wondering how all these diagrams directly relate to coaching. Well, let me make this explicitly clear.

> "Success is a science;
> if you have the conditions, you get the results."
> Oscar Wilde

The ThinkOn® Results Framework provides the conditions for success and is as scientific as we need to get without delving into a study of how the brain works and how thoughts eventually become actions.

If we know that there are simple, logical principles that we unconsciously use when we are successful, then these can be combined into a structured framework and flexible questioning process. This can then be used to coach yourself or others in order to deliberately improve the probability of achieving what we consciously set out to achieve.

TIME TO REFLECT

Before continuing to read further, just pause to reflect on your learning so far. Consider the following questions:

What is the most significant realisation I have had so far about making a difference?

How can I use this when coaching myself or others?

What have I discovered about coaching?

What is ThinkOn®?

How confident am I in my ability to remember, draw, or explain the ThinkOn® Results Framework?

Have I actually written in this book yet?

How strong is my reason for developing my coaching skills?

PART TWO: LINKING THINKON® WITH HIGH QUALITY QUESTIONS

16. The answers are on the inside

Coaching is definitely not about telling people what they should do. It is about helping individuals to become aware of their current situation, abilities and possibilities and encouraging them to take personal responsibility for making the difference they want to make. The most effective way of doing this is to stimulate their thoughts by asking them high quality questions.

> "The answers are on the inside and the role of the coach is to unlock them from the outside."
> Andy Gilbert

Helping people to understand through the skillful use of questioning, instead of attempting to make them understand through telling, creates deeper levels of understanding and self-awareness. It allows the individual to choose their thoughts and take responsibility for their choices. Telling or giving advice, however well meaning, denies that choice.

Good questioning allows individuals to resolve issues for themselves and challenges habitual ways of thinking and behaving. It helps people to generate their own answers and have ownership of the way forward. This in turn generates greater commitment to taking action. It also prevents the individual from blaming the coach, because no advice has been given.

As a ThinkOn® coach it is not my responsibility to have technical knowledge or expertise in a specific topic other than the ThinkOn® Key Principles and their systemic relationship. I do take responsibility, however, for asking good questions to help the individual to focus on where to find information – either within themselves or by involving others.

17. What is a high quality question?

The answer, in very simple terms, is one that generates a high quality answer or thought. As a coach, the purpose of asking high quality questions is to help the people you are coaching to generate high quality answers in order to help themselves.

"No problem can withstand the assault of sustained thinking."
Voltaire

Higher quality questions get higher quality answers. So, what makes a question high quality?

Notice the question I have asked you. This is an example of a high quality question. There is no obvious, easy "yes/no" response or a simple factual answer – it causes you to think. Said out loud, this question is also an example of linguistic ambiguity in that it can be said as the following statement:

"What" – makes a question high quality!

Interestingly it also contains an answer to the previous question, i.e. the use of the word "what" at the start can create a high quality question. I estimate that between 60-70% of the questions I ask when coaching start with the word, "What".

The next most common word I use to begin my high quality coaching questions is, "How". Approximately 20-25% of my questions start with this word.

Questions that start with, "How" and "What" are often referred to as open questions. This means that they cannot be answered "yes" or "no", and therefore require a more open response. Open questions therefore require a person to think more deeply. Examples of open questions that I commonly use at the start of a coaching session are:

- What specifically do you want to make a difference about?

- How strong is your reason why for wanting to make this difference?

- How will you measure your success?

- What is the underlying reason for seeking to change?

When training people to become ThinkOn® Coaches I often use mental imagery to help them remember key points. Here is one for you to consider:

Picture in your mind a boxing ring in a gymnasium. The room is full of boxers training hard – pummelling punch bags and shadow boxing. In the ring is a boxer sparring with a partner. In the corner is the trainer – a much older, experienced person – shouting instructions. The instructions consist of only a few words, repeated over and over again. "Duck and dive! Duck and dive! Bob and weave! Bob and weave!" The boxer continues to box; the trainer continues to shout. The same words are repeated once more, "Bob and weave, duck and dive!" The boxer starts to move in accordance with the instructions and still the trainer continues to shout the same few words.

Now imagine coaching someone, asking high quality questions. Inside your head you hear a voice reminding you of how to phrase them. "What and how; what and what; what and how!" Remind yourself over and over that these two words will form the start of the majority of your high quality coaching questions.

"**What and how; what and how; what and how.**"
ThinkOn® coaches everywhere

However, there is more to a high quality question than just the word it starts with. There are several other important factors to consider. Each question must be relevant to the ThinkOn® Results Framework i.e. its purpose is to help the other person consider the difference they want to make in relation to either a ThinkOn® Key Principle or one of the links. Any person observing the coaching session should easily be able to identify which part of the ThinkOn® Results Framework the coach is questioning about.

High quality questions are predominantly future and solution focused. They keep the individual focused on the difference they say they want to make. Sometimes individuals want to talk about the past difficulties they have experienced and to indulge in a bit of blaming. A good coach will be supportive, yet challenging, to keep the person focused on what will help them.

Example

Individual:"Whenever I start to make progress, something urgent seems to crop up that isn't my fault. Last week, for example, when Peter interrupted me. He didn't realise that...."

50

Coach (interrupting): "Rather than dwell on the past, let's focus on the difference you want to make in the next few weeks. What possible steps could you take towards achieving your goal?"

ThinkOn® coaching is unlike a normal day-to-day conversation because the coach has to resist natural curiosity about incidents that have happened. Instead, the attention must be entirely focused on helping the other person move forward.

"Waste no tears over the griefs of yesterday."
Euripides

The final aspect of a high quality question is that it encourages the individual to focus on specific detail. For example, rather than asking a general question such as, "How much help do you want from others?" a more specific, higher quality question would be, "What specific help would be of most use to you, that others could provide?"

18. Essential stuff to know about the different types of questions

There are six words commonly used at the start of an open question. These are what, how, who, when, where and why. As I mentioned in the previous chapter the most useful coaching questions start with, "what" and "how". It will also be necessary to ask some "who" questions relating to principle five (involve others) e.g. "Who could you possibly involve to help you achieve your goal? Who will you involve first?"

Notice how these questions will identify specific individuals or groups of people. Questions that start with the words "who," "when" or "where" are sometimes referred to as a subset of open questions known as specific open questions. They will elicit information about people (who), places (where) and timescales (when). All are used in ThinkOn® coaching to a limited extent when defining the goal (principle two), and considering possibilities (principles three and five). It is only when focusing attention on the individual taking responsibility (principle six) that the coach invites the individual to make choices about who to involve, when to take action, where to go and ultimately what to do.

"A prudent question is one-half of wisdom."
Francis Bacon

Avoid using questions starting with the word "why." It can easily be interpreted as confrontational or accusatory. "Why" questions tend to elicit excuses, reasons and justifications which are not useful in helping to develop high quality thinking. Hence good coaches avoid asking them. "Why" questions can always be softened by replacing the "why" with a "what", for example: "What are the reasons for...?" or, "What causes you to believe that?"

The opposite of open questions are closed questions, i.e. questions that elicit a "yes/no" response. Throughout coaching these are usually avoided as they are generally not high quality in helping the other person to think deeply enough. If too many closed questions are being asked it means that the person attempting to coach is doing most of the thinking and the talking!

Here are a couple of things to watch out for and avoid:

–   Leading or judgmental questions: For example, "Don't you think you should consider making time to do the important tasks?" This really means, "I think you should spend more time doing the important tasks and I want you to agree with me!" Even more unsubtle and clumsy is the leading question that starts, "Wouldn't you agree that...?" Definitely not a high quality question! Remember that, as a coach, your role is to help the other person think for themselves – not to lead them.

"The doorstep to the temple of wisdom is a knowledge of our own ignorance."
Benjamin Franklin

–   Multiple questions: For example, "What difference do you want to make, how strong is your reason for wanting it and what are some of the possible obstacles to consider?" This presents three questions in one sentence and is likely to overwhelm the person on the receiving end. People will usually only answer the last, or easiest, part of a multiple question. Separately, the three questions are good open, high quality questions. However, without pausing to allow an answer to the first question, what started as a high quality question becomes a poor quality multiple question.

It is okay to deliberately ask closed questions in order to obtain a yes/no response, if that is what you are seeking to do. I estimate that 5-10% of my coaching questions are closed. Examples of when to do this include when you deliberately want to check your understanding and when you want to check that a person is prepared to be accountable for making the difference they say they are going to make.

19. Two types of high quality question

The two types of H.Q.Q. (High Quality Question) relate to their purpose; questions that engage the imagination to open the mind and questions that focus the mind. Both types are important and are used at various stages of ThinkOn® coaching.

Questions that focus the mind are predominately used to help the individual: assess motivation and self-belief; define goals/sub-goals; make choices; plan priorities; and take personal responsibility.

Every question must have a purpose and be directly relevant to either one of the key principles or one of the links between them. The diagram below illustrates the areas of the framework where it is useful for coaches to ask H.Q.Q.'s that focus the mind.

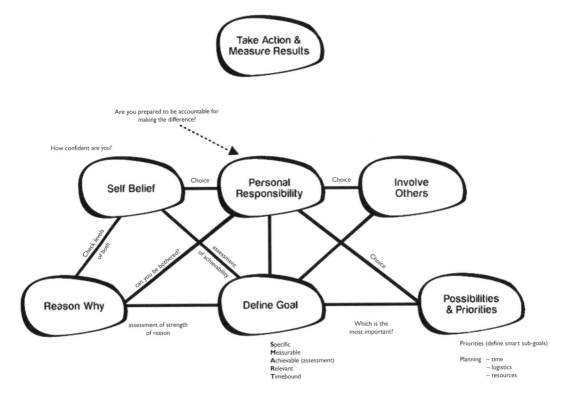

Questions that engage the imagination are mainly used to: visualise future success; generate possibilities; create break-throughs in thinking; and strengthen self-belief.

The following diagram illustrates the key principles, and links between them, where ThinkOn® coaches commonly ask H.Q.Q.'s that engage the imagination.

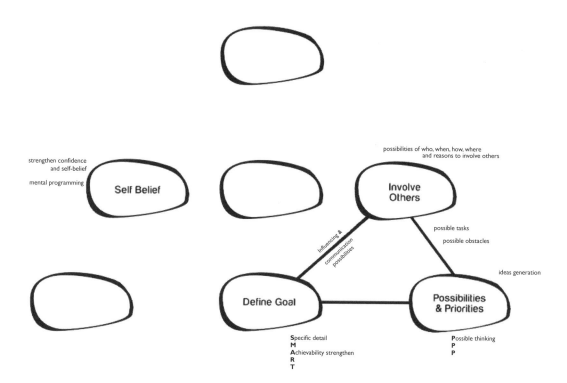

In Part Three of this book there are plenty of H.Q.Q. examples for you to study and select favourites from.

20. Every question has a purpose

Let's recap some of the main points so far and piece them together to understand the importance of questioning as the critical skill used in ThinkOn® coaching. We know that there are seven Key Success Principles, the first six of which form a robust coaching framework comprising 11 links. Furthermore, the ThinkOn® Results Framework encompasses over 26 competency areas that can be individually developed in order to help a person make a measurable difference.

The key to successful ThinkOn® coaching is to ensure that every question you ask is directly relevant to either one of the key principles or one of the links between them.

By following the ThinkOn® Results Framework in your mind you will soon learn to move easily from one part to another. If you are coaching a person or a team who is familiar with ThinkOn®, you can draw the framework as you coach them. This really does keep questions focused. Remember the purpose of your questioning is to help others develop their ability to make a difference. By asking H.Q.Q.'s relevant to each part of the framework you will do this.

"The secret of success is constancy of purpose."
Benjamin Disraeli

The ThinkOn® Results Framework will provide you with a consistent approach to coaching once you apply your H.Q.Q.'s to it. Every part of the framework has its purpose, hence every question must do the same.

21. Control the system, not the content

Your responsibility as a coach is to be consciously aware of which part of the ThinkOn® system you are helping the other person to think about. Think of yourself as a systems thinking consultant and remain detached from the content of what the other person is saying – however interesting it might be!

Even now, after many years of experience of coaching, I often find it easier to coach someone when I know nothing about the subject. Remember that coaching in its purist sense is not about teaching, advising, sharing knowledge or problem solving. It is easy for inexperienced managers and people new to coaching to get sucked into the situation. I call this "content seduction", and, in the past, I have fallen into the content seduction trap many times.

> "It is a mistake to aim to get inside the other person. Coaching is about standing next to the person and helping them to see and understand the reality for themselves."
> Andy Gilbert

The coach is responsible for using good coaching skills and applying the ThinkOn® system; the individual is responsible for their own thoughts and development actions.

22. Content free coaching

A powerful exercise that I often use on coaching programmes, and when conference speaking, is to simultaneously coach the entire group or audience (sometimes several hundred at the same time). My questions cannot be answered out loud (or else chaos would ensue), so I request that people write their response. In effect, I am coaching blind – in that I am unable to see the impact that my coaching is having – other than observing the group writing their answers. After the demonstration I ask how many people have benefited from this 25-30 minute exercise and always obtain a positive response of over 95%.

(There is always a small percentage who do not fully participate because of either low self-belief or a lack of a strong reason why to make a difference.)

The impact of this demonstration is often amazing as people start to understand how the ThinkOn® system can be applied to coach others without any knowledge or understanding of the difference they want to make.

"The real voyage of discovery consists not in seeking new landscapes, but in having new eyes."
Marcel Proust

---

23. A 40 question coaching script

Imagine that you are attending a conference where I am about to do the exercise I described in the previous chapter. The following 40 questions are ones that I might use if I was coaching you. If you are serious about making a difference, then please get a pen and a pad of paper and get ready to start writing. Now I realise that it is tempting just to scan through these questions. However, I guarantee that if you spend 30-40 minutes, writing your answers to each question, you will improve your ability to make a difference.

1. What specifically do you want to achieve? (i.e. what difference do you want to make?)

2. What is your precise measure of success? (i.e. how will you know when you have achieved your goal?)

3. What exact date will you achieve this by?

4. How achievable do you believe this goal to be? (Note: on a scale of 1 (low) to 10 (high) if you assess it to be 5 or less, then redefine the goal to make it more achievable.)

5. How relevant is this goal to what is important to you in life? (i.e. check it doesn't conflict with any other priorities.)

6. What are the reasons why you want to make this difference?

7. How strong is your motivation to achieve your defined goal? (Note: if it is not strong, then choose something else to make a difference about.)

8. What possible tasks could help you to make the difference you desire? (Note: start making a list of possibilities.)

9. What resources could possibly help you?

10. What possible help could benefit you?

11. Who could possibly help you?

12. How could they possibly help you?

13. What other possibilities could you consider? (Note: include possible obstacles, risks and ways of overcoming them. Be creative in your thinking and remember you are only listing ideas - not evaluating them.)

14. Who else could possibly help?

15. What could you possibly gain from involving others?

16. How could you influence others to help you?

17. What might be the most effective way of persuading them?

18. What are the possible implications?

19. Who else could you involve? (Note: think laterally about how and where you can access people that have knowledge/skills but don't even know you!)

20. What else could you possibly do that might be helpful in achieving your goal? (Note: keep adding to your list.)

21. What else?

22. Which of the possibilities are your priorities? (i.e. those that are most important to the achievement of your goal.)

23. What is your top priority?

24. What areas need to be broken down into smaller tasks?

25. When do these need to be achieved by? (Note: convert your priority actions into specific, measurable, time bound goals.)

26. How will you ensure you set aside sufficient time to work on achieving your sub-goal priorities? (Note: actually plan these activities into your diary by blocking out time.)

27. Who will you choose to involve?

28. How will you involve them and obtain their commitment?

29. By when? (Note: plan in the time to do it.)

30. How strong is your self-belief that your goal is achievable?

31. What potential obstacles are you likely to encounter?

32. What will be your greatest challenge in achieving this goal?

33. What can you do to further develop your self-belief?

34. How strong is your reason why you want to make this difference?

35. What choices have you got to make?

36. How accountable are you prepared to be for making it happen?

37. How willing are you to take personal responsibility (i.e. without blaming anyone/anything) for making the difference you say you want to make?

38. How will you review and measure your results?

39. How will you celebrate your success?

40. When are you going to start to take action?

Notice, as you complete this exercise, which questions cause you to think more deeply. By the end of this book you will have developed your understanding of which questions to ask and in what order. The good news is that you don't have to memorise them! Keep reading and you will discover ways of how to ask the right question at the right time.

TIME TO REFLECT

Having completed this exercise, consider the following questions:

What benefit have I gained?

Which questions were the most helpful?

What have I realised about developing my ability to make a difference?

What have I realised about applying the ThinkOn® Results Framework?

24. The sound of silence

As a coach you need to become comfortable with the silences that may occur.

"Those in a hurry, do not arrive."
Zen saying

People need time to think and arrive at their own conclusions. I have observed many people practising their coaching skills who ask a great H.Q.Q. and then do not allow enough time for the person they are coaching to think. They break the silence by asking another question which has the effect of creating a multiple question.

I often get asked about how long to leave a silence for and what to do in the silence. My advice is to observe the other person. In particular their eyes and mouth, as these two areas will give you lots of clues. For example, do you get the impression that they are thinking, looking for inspiration and searching within themselves for an answer? Or, are you picking up clues that they are stuck and need further help? Occasionally I might break a long silence to ask a question like, "What are you thinking?" or, "What are some of your thoughts?"

25. Being creative with H.Q.Q.'s

As long as your questions are high quality with the purpose of helping the individual think through the framework, you can be as creative as you wish in constructing them. This is particularly appropriate for the type of H.Q.Q.'s that are designed to engage the imagination in generating possibilities. (Part Three contains several examples.) If a question does not elicit an appropriate response, ask another question. A technique I occasionally use is to ask the individual to generate their own questions, for example I ask:

"What is the real question you need to answer before you move forward?"

"What is the important question you have avoided asking yourself?"

"What is the one question that, if you answered it, would help you the most?"

Watch out at this point, because there is usually a huge silence! The reason for this is that in answering your question, the individual has to generate and evaluate several questions in their own mind and probably start to consider the answers to them. This will take more than a couple of seconds.

"To ask the hard question is simple."
W. H. Auden

---

26. Case study example

The following example is an extract from a coaching session I recorded. After approximately five minutes we had a well-defined goal about a work related project and had started to explore possibilities (principle three). I observed the individual had started to hesitate and be less decisive in her answers to my questions when this happened:

Individual: "I'm stuck. I'm not sure what to do."

Andy: "That's okay. What's the one question that, if you answered it, would help you to become unstuck?"

Individual (responding immediately): "I don't know!"

Andy: "That's okay. Just take your time and imagine that you do know what that important question is that needs answering."

Individual (after a long silence): "I do know what the question is, because I've been thinking about it a lot."

Andy: "What is it?"

Individual: "Am I in the right job?"

Andy: "And what's the answer?"

Individual: "No, I'm not. I want to move into another department."

Andy: "How important is that to you?"

Individual: "Very! I think about it all day!"

Andy: "Which is the most important to you – completing the project or moving department?"

Individual: "Moving department. I know I can complete the project on time, but I'm unhappy in my job."

Andy: "So, do you want to take personal responsibility for doing something about it?"

Individual: "Definitely, but I don't know how."

Andy: "Let's leave the how until later. For the moment, let's focus on defining what you want."

Individual: "Okay."

This is a typical example of how a coaching session about making a difference in one area can change when a stronger reason why emerges. Let's analyse that previous coaching dialogue in more detail and I will share with you my observations.

Individual: "I'm stuck. I'm not sure what to do."

At this point I interpreted that the individual, from her behaviour, including her vocal tone and body language, was indirectly asking me for help. Her self-belief (principle four) had changed from earlier in the conversation and she had now moved from being confident to "stuck."

Andy: "That's okay. What's the one question that, if you answered it, would help you to become unstuck?"

The first thing I did was to reassure her that being stuck is okay. I then had a number of options to consider. If I asked the question, "What are you stuck about?" or, "What is causing you to be stuck?", I could elicit a possible lengthy response about either the problem or the past. As ThinkOn® coaching is solution focused and future orientated, this would not be helpful (it is always an option to stop coaching and adopt a counselling approach). I decided to ask a H.Q.Q. that contained within it the presupposition that if she could identify one question and answer it, then she would become unstuck. I deliberately used the word "unstuck" as the desired outcome I presumed she was seeking.

Individual (responding immediately): "I don't know!"

There was no attempt to answer the question because she still believed that she was stuck - and people always act in accordance with their beliefs. I realised that I needed to ask a H.Q.Q. that engaged her imagination and reassure her that it was okay not to know — yet.

Andy: "That's okay. Just take your time and imagine that you do know what that important question is that needs answering."

Notice that I did not actually ask a question. Instead I gave an instruction that followed on from the reassurance, i.e. I told her to imagine that she does know. I then paused and observed.

Individual (after a long silence): "I do know what the question is, because I've been thinking about it a lot."

Hurray! I believed she would come up with something, if I just caused her to think about the underlying reason for being stuck.

Andy: "What is it?"

The obvious question to ask.

Individual: "Am I in the right job?"

I interpreted her tone of voice and facial expression as an indication of seriousness about this issue. I was unaware of what job this person did and resisted the temptation to get content seduced.

Andy: "And what's the answer?"

A simple, short, open question.

Individual: "No, I'm not. I want to move into another department."

Her answer was very decisive – an indication that she had perhaps known this for a while. My thoughts now moved back to the framework and I started to test the strength of her reason why (principle one).

Andy: "How important is that to you?"

This question is linked to her personal values.

Individual: "Very! I think about it all day!"

The speed and intensity of her response gave me a more balanced assessment of the strength of her reason – not just the words of her answer.

Andy: "Which is the most important to you – completing the project or moving department?"

I was aware that there were two issues that we were focusing on and, as a coach, I needed to understand which one took priority so I could focus the coaching on the most important.

Individual: "Moving department. I know I can complete the project on time, but I'm unhappy in my job."

A decisive answer and indication of high self-belief about the original goal. Plus, I also discovered that the reason why relating to moving jobs is away motivated, i.e. to move away from being unhappy in her current job. I made a mental note of this to refer back to, if necessary, at a later stage of the coaching (the check line).

Andy: "So, do you want to take personal responsibility for doing something about it?"

A deliberate closed question (moving from reason why on the ThinkOn® Results Framework along the choice line to personal responsibility) to find out if she was serious enough about making a difference.

Individual: "Definitely, but I don't know how."

This low self-belief was the cause of her being stuck. She had a strong reason why, but had bypassed defining a goal and was worrying about the how. This is quite typical of differences that are based on away motivation; she knew what she didn't want, but hadn't defined what she did want.

Andy: "Let's leave the how until later. For the moment, let's focus on defining what you want."

As the coach I am responsible for controlling the structure of the coaching session and ensuring that a goal is clearly defined before considering how possibly to make a difference. The person being coached is responsible for choosing the goal. What started as coaching about project management ended as coaching about career management – the content/subject of the coaching is for the individual to choose.

Individual: "Okay."

Indicated an acceptance of trusting the coach with the process.

TIME TO REFLECT

Consider the following questions:

What have I realised from studying this case study example?

What do I want to learn more about?

27. A blank page

Well, not quite a blank page! Before I describe the classic way of structuring sequences of questions to follow the ThinkOn® Results Framework, please take the opportunity to practise drawing the framework below. How many of the key principles, and links between them, can you recall?

28. The classic ThinkOn® coaching route

This chapter is not about understanding what questions to ask; this chapter is about understanding how to use the ThinkOn® Results Framework in order to effectively structure a sequence of coaching questions.

When I am coaching I never prepare or use a set of standard questions. However, a couple of questions that I commonly use at the start of a coaching session are:

"How serious are you about wanting to make a difference?"

"What difference do you want to make?"

Notice that the first question relates to principle one and the second question is focused on identifying the goal (principle two). With ThinkOn® coaching you can start with either *why* a person wants to make a difference or *what* the difference is that they want to make. Either is okay.

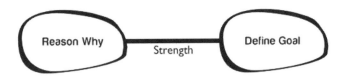

If I start with the why, I then move onto the what. Alternatively if I start with defining what the difference is, I then move back to identifying the strength of the underlying reason for wanting to make that difference. Once the individual has taken personal responsibility for identifying their motivation to change, assessed the strength of that motivation and defined a SMART goal, then it is time to move on.

The following diagram illustrates the elements of the framework that have been completed at this stage.

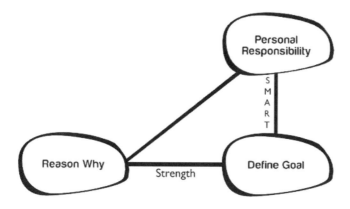

As part of the process in defining a SMART goal, I usually ask a question like, "On a scale of 1-10, how high is your self-belief that the goal will be achieved by the date you set?"

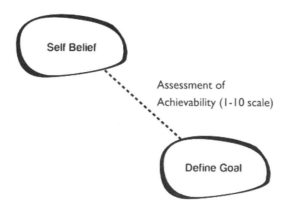

If the score is six or more I proceed onto the third key principle. However, if the score is five or less I recognise that there is a greater amount of self-doubt than there is self-belief. I now have a couple of choices. I can either ask questions to explore the limiting beliefs about the goal and then amend the goal, or develop another goal related to increasing self-belief. If the goal is amended to be more achievable in terms of what the difference will be within a realistic timescale, the individual's self-belief will increase. Once the self-belief level is at least a six out of ten, I can continue following the ThinkOn® Results Framework in the usual way. In chapter 14, I referred to "working the triangles," and I always start with the first triangle.

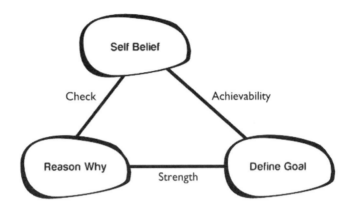

Once this triangle is solid, I can move onto working the second triangle.

There are three elements to principle three – the three P's – the first of which is possibilities. I now ask a series of H.Q.Q.'s designed to help the person think about, and identify a long list of possibilities. In our original research we identified ten generic possibility thinking areas which people commonly thought about (see chapters 47 & 48). Using these ten areas as a basis for my questions, I sometimes repeat the same question several times to stimulate ideas about possible tasks, possible people to involve and how to possibly obtain their buy-in. Once the other person is thinking in terms of possibilities it needs little more than to ask, "What else? Who else? How else?" in a variety of ways.

Eventually, after working two sides of this triangle (the task and buy-in lines), I move onto the importance line and invite the person to identify their priorities, which includes choosing who to definitely involve. I then ask a series of H.Q.Q.'s to convert these priorities into SMART sub-goals.

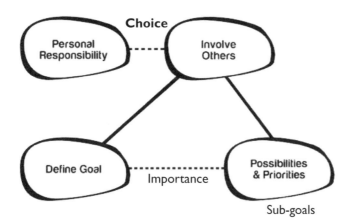

Once these sub-goals have been defined I return to assess the level of self-belief relating to the achievement of the original goal (see diagram on next page). If it has fallen, then I question to establish if the goal needs to be redefined or the individual wants to take personal responsibility for developing their self-belief in other ways.

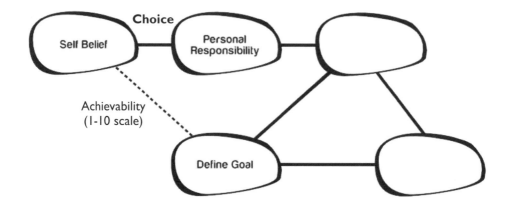

If the level of self-belief is still high then I move down the check line to question if the motivation/reason why is still as strong. The following diagram illustrates the links that have now been completed.

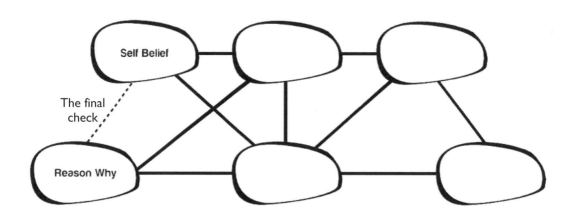

Once this has been checked, I return to personal responsibility and the link with possibilities & priorities. The third P is about planning in time to do the priorities, and challenging the individual being coached to do exactly that.

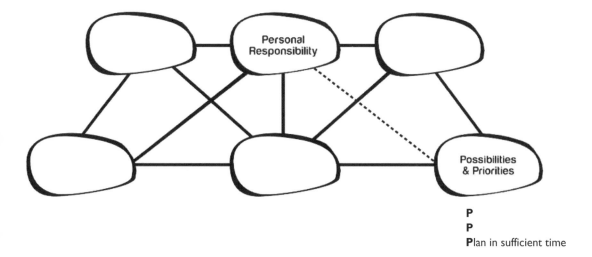

Personal
Responsibility

Possibilities
& Priorities

P
P
Plan in sufficient time

Once they have allocated time in their diary/planning system to take action on their priorities, I keep the person focused on personal responsibility to consider the implications of being accountable and a role model for others.

Finally I ask a few questions about taking action, measuring results and ensuring the momentum is maintained. H.Q.Q.'s, to engage the imagination, are often used to help visualise future success.

The route around the ThinkOn® Results Framework I have just described, is the most common and time efficient one I use when coaching.

29. Using alternative routes

Occasionally, as in the case study example (chapter 26), the person you are coaching may decide that they want to focus on something else. At any time, when working the second (external) triangle, you must be prepared to return to work the first (internal) triangle. Remember that the framework is a system – not a process – and hence you must decide which part of the system will require immediate focus.

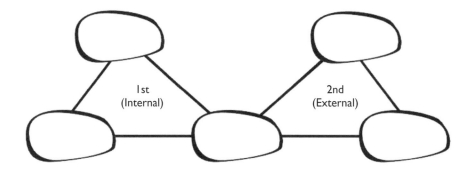

You might notice, whilst coaching, that the self-belief is dropping or the reason why does not appear to be as strong. If this happens, then stop doing whatever you are doing in the system and return to the relevant key principle. Ask H.Q.Q.'s to focus the person on assessing the achievability link and determining the strength of their motivation. If the goal needs to be redefined or swapped, then do it.

"Everything should be made as simple as possible, but not simpler."
Albert Einstein

As a coach you are working to ensure that the person is simply applying each Key Principle and that there are strong links between them.

30. A shorter "blind" coaching script

The following questions and instructions (in italics) were given as a blind coaching exercise on a recent training course. The session was recorded and then the sequence of the questions was analysed to identify how closely it followed the classic ThinkOn® coaching routeway.

Question	Structure
1. What difference do you want to make?	Define Goal
2. What specifically do you want to achieve and by what date?	Define Goal (specific, timescale)
3. How exactly will you measure the difference when you have made it?	Define Goal (measurable)
4. What is your defined goal in a single sentence?	Define Goal
5. How strong is your reason for wanting to achieve this, in comparison with other things happening in your life?	Reason Why (strength) Define Goal (relevant)
6. How achievable do you believe this goal to be? *Measure it on a scale of 1-10.*	Self-Belief Define Goal (achievable)
7. What are some of the possible things you could do to help you achieve this goal?	Possibility Thinking (1st stage of Possibilities & Priorities)
8. What else might possibly help?	Possibility Thinking
9. What resources might be useful?	Possibility Thinking
10. How could others possibly help you?	Possibility Thinking
11. What other reasons might there be to involve others? *Remember these are just possibilities.*	Possibility Thinking
12. Who could you possibly involve?	Possibility Thinking
13. Who else could possibly add value and help in some way?	Possibility Thinking
14. How could you possibly communicate your goal to others in order to obtain their support?	Possibility Thinking (buy-in)
15. What else could you possibly do to influence others and gain their "buy-in" to your goal?	Possibility Thinking
16. Who else could you involve? *Stretch yourself to think wider.*	Possibility Thinking
17. What possible obstacles might you encounter in working towards achieving your goal?	Possibility Thinking
18. What else might steer you off course or possibly prevent you from being successful?	Possibility Thinking

19. What possible risks or implications might be useful to consider?	Possibility Thinking
20. How could you possibly overcome any obstacles or reduce any possible risks?	Possibility Thinking
21. Who could possibly help you?	Possibility Thinking
22. What possible assumptions might you be making?	Possibility Thinking
23. How might you be imposing limitations on yourself?	Possibility Thinking
24. What other possibilities are there for achieving what you want to achieve?	Possibility Thinking
25. What are the most important things to consider or do from your list of possibilities? *Underline or highlight them.*	Priorities (importance)
26. Which of these priorities is the most important? *Decide exactly what you will do by what date.*	Priorities
27. For each priority decide specifically, what you will do and by when?	Sub-goals (choices)
28. Who will you definitely involve and how?	Priorities (involve others)
29. How achievable do you believe your original goal to be? *Again, use a scale of 1-10.*	Self-Belief (check)
30. *If you don't believe it is achievable (less than 6) review your reason why and goal. Question what is stopping you and consider possibilities about that potential obstacle.*	Review Internal Triangle
31. How strong is your desire to achieve this goal?	Reason Why (check)
32. Are you prepared to be accountable for achieving this goal?	Personal Responsibility
33. What time will you set aside in order to achieve your priorities?	Plan Priorities (choice)
34. A challenge – *if you have a diary/planner with you, write in reminders or block out time.*	Plan Priorities (choice)
35. How will you measure your progress?	Personal Responsibility (choice)
36. How will you celebrate your success?	End

31. A pause to reflect on learning so far

Section Three of this book focuses in more detail on each of the ThinkOn® Key Principles and contains useful information, tips and techniques relevant to each stage of the coaching process.

"The only thing that matters is how you touch people.
Have I given anyone insight?
That's what I want to have done.
Insight lasts: theories don't."
Peter Drucker

TIME TO REFLECT

Before you delve into the detail of the following section, just pause to reflect on your learning from this section. Consider the following questions:

What have I discovered about asking high quality questions?

How can I use this when coaching myself or others?

What have I realised about coaching?

What have I realised about my own ability to make a difference?

What have I learned about using the ThinkOn® Results Framework for coaching?

What else have I discovered?

PART THREE: THE THINKON® RESULTS FRAMEWORK IN GREATER DETAIL

The ThinkOn® Results Framework, when applied to coaching, can easily be divided into eight sections: identifying the strength of reason why; defining the goal; generating possibilities; deciding priorities; building confidence; action planning; testing commitment; and agreeing the way forward. Whilst they might not necessarily happen in this exact order (e.g. sometimes the goal is defined before the reason why is considered, and sometimes confidence needs to be built before possibilities are explored), this is perhaps the most logical order to explore the ThinkOn® Results Framework in greater detail.

SECTION ONE

32. Identifying the strength of reason why – key points

One of the initial tasks of the coach is to help the individual be consciously aware of his or her level of motivation. Establishing this strength of purpose or underlying reason why the person wants to make a difference is essential in the coaching session. The number of reasons is not important; the strength of reason is critical.

> "Great minds have purposes,
> others have wishes."
> Washington Irving

Here are some key points to bear in mind at this stage:

- the reason why to make a difference has to be stronger than the reason not to make a difference in order for action to be taken.

- people will either be motivated towards something they desire or motivated away from something they don't want.

- it is useful to know whether the person you are coaching is towards or away from motivated.

- only when the pain of the situation is greater than the gain of being in that situation, will the reason why be sufficiently strong.

- if a person is away motivated, then their reason why is likely to decrease as they start to move away from the pain, i.e. things become more comfortable. Hence the need to have a future focused goal if further differences are to be made.

- the person you are coaching is likely to have a different reason for making a difference than you have.

- the strongest reasons for making a difference are those that are the core values of that person.

33. High quality questions to ask

Very often the reason a person is seeking to make a difference will already be known or be obvious to you. Be careful about asking too many questions at this stage of the coaching session. As a coach you only need to establish the strength of their reason why. Dependent upon how well you know the person, their strength of reason might already be apparent. Hence, there might be no need to ask any questions, at this point, if you are aware of a strong underlying reason why this person wants to make a difference.

For most of my coaching sessions, I tend to ask only a couple of reason why questions at the start, sometimes after the goal has been defined, together with a final strength check towards the end. Here are a selection to stimulate your thinking and add to:

- what is your reason for wanting to make a difference?

- how strong is your reason on a scale of 1-10?

- what makes it that strong?

- how important is it for you to change your current situation?

- what is the single most important reason for wanting this?

- what are you prepared to sacrifice in order to achieve your goal?

- what are the implications of doing nothing?

- how much do you want to be successful in making this difference?

- what is important to you about achieving this goal?

- how relevant will this difference be to the things that matter most?

- how strong is your desire to succeed?

- how will it make you happy?

- how will it improve your current situation?

- how much do you honestly want it?

- what would be a stronger reason for not doing it?

- what would happen if you didn't make it happen?

- what is motivating you to want to make a difference?

- what will you gain?

- how valuable will this achievement be?

- what is it that causes you to want to do this?

- what will make it worth the effort?

- what is the single driving factor that will keep you going?

- how willing are you to change?

- how prepared are you to do what it takes?

- what makes you feel so strongly about this?

- on a scale of 1-10, how much does this matter to you?

- what is the difference this will make on a personal level?

- how important is this goal in relation to the other priorities in your life?

- how passionate are you about this difference that you say you want to make?

- how important is it to you on a scale of 1-10?

- what is the reason that makes this difference worthwhile?

- what is causing you to want this?

- how serious are you?

- what is the significance of this timescale?

- what will success give you that you haven't already got?

- what will you do with the money? (i.e. to identify the underlying reasons why money is important.)

- what's in it for you?

- what's in it for your team?

- what's in it for your organisation?

- what are the consequences of not making a difference?

- is the reason why strong enough to sustain the time and effort?

34. Linking the Reason Why with other ThinkOn® Key Principles

There are three links between the first ThinkOn® Key Principle and others in the framework.

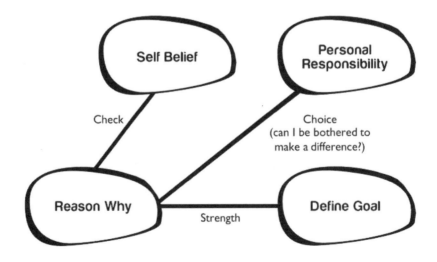

The first of these is the choice line that links with the key principle of taking personal responsibility. An effective coach, through the use of H.Q.Q.'s, encourages an individual to take responsibility for assessing their personal motivation and determining whether or not it is strong enough to underpin the defined goal. In answering the coaching questions the individual is choosing to take that responsibility. The underlying question relating to personal choice is, "Can I be bothered to make a difference?"

The link with having a defined goal is obvious. It doesn't matter how well defined the goal is; without a sufficiently strong reason why that goal is worthwhile for the individual, the goal will not be achieved. When defining a goal, it is important to ensure that it is relevant to the values of the individual or the organisation. Hence the use of questions that explore the relevance or importance of the difference to what the organisation or person values.

> "It is not enough to be busy, so are the ants.
> The question is, what are we busy about?"
> Henry David Thoreau

The check line provides the link between motivation (reason why) and confidence (self-belief). In order to succeed, the individual needs both in sufficient strength. Towards the end of each ThinkOn® coaching session I always ask a question to check this. It is usually phrased in the form of an instruction, e.g. "Now that you have identified your priorities and how much time you need to plan in order to achieve your goal, just check how strong your reason is for still wanting to make that difference."

35. What to watch out for: reason why

It's not just the answer to your question that you are waiting for. Vital clues about the strength of peoples' motivation can be gained from their vocal tone and body language. In other words, it's not what they say - but how they say it. The speed, volume and pitch of the response are all important and might warrant the asking of further questions to challenge or explore what was said.

When using a 1-10 scale in an assessment question, watch out for people who over-assess the strength of their reason for making a difference. Sometimes people say they are serious about making a difference when they are not. Watch out for, and challenge, key words that indicate this. "I'll try," indicates either a lack of confidence, motivation or commitment, as does, "I will...one day." A good coach would reflect these comments back to the person and invite them to make a choice whether or not to make a difference.

---

*"Words may show a man's wit
but actions his meaning."*
Benjamin Franklin

Watch out for confident people with a high self-belief but a low reason why. They could make a difference, but can't be bothered; they are likely to waste your time when coaching them.

Sometimes people can get carried away when describing their reasons for wanting to make a difference. Occasionally this explanation reveals an underlying problem that the individual wants to explain in great detail, believing that this will help the coach to understand. An effective coach will intervene to shift the focus away from the past towards defining the desired future.

---

*"Dwelling on the difficulties does not move you
forward. The cause of past problems rarely
contributes to future success."*
Andy Gilbert

And finally, just because you might know a person, you might not know their latest thinking or current circumstances. An individual's motivation to make a difference can change quite dramatically as a result of changing life experiences. Remember that a high quality question is always better than an assumption.

TIME TO REFLECT

Having reached the end of this section, consider the following questions:

What have I realised about the significance of motivation within the ThinkOn® system?
What will I be aware of when asking H.Q.Q.'s about the strength of a person's reason why?
Which questions do I like the most from chapter 33?
What questions of my own can I add?
What else have I realised?

SECTION TWO

36. The importance of defining the goal

This part of the ThinkOn® system will initially happen as the first activity or, as the second part of the coaching session, once the strength of the reason why has been assessed. Once the difference has been defined it might need to be subsequently amended to reflect a changing self-belief or to obtain buy-in from others. The ability to skillfully help people define goals is also relevant when converting priorities into sub-goals and is an essential part of becoming an effective coach.

> "One day Alice came to a fork in the road
> and saw a Cheshire cat in a tree.
> "Which road do I take?" she asked.
> His response was a question:
> "Where do you want to go?"
> **Lewis Carroll**

The everyday equivalent of this Alice in Wonderland quote happens whenever people focus on how to do something before defining what the specific difference is they want to make. The greatest coach in the world cannot help a person make a difference if that person cannot first define what the difference is!

37. Defining the goal – key points

Many organisations, and people working within them, use a similar process to help teams and individuals define goals and business objectives. One of the most commonly used acronyms for doing this is SMART. I estimate that, in most of the large organisations I work with, approximately ninety percent of managers have either heard of SMART or know what word each initial represents (Specific, Measurable, Achievable, Relevant, Timescale).

However, I have discovered that less than ten percent have developed the ability to actually write a basic SMART goal in a single sentence. Before I reveal how to do this, and how to help others do the same, I will first outline some key points to bear in mind:

- Goals focus on what you want, rather than what you don't want.

- Goals are specific in their detail; whereas aims are vague.

- Goals are measurable in either time, cost, quantity or quality; whereas aims cannot be measured.

- Individuals have to believe that their goals are achievable within the defined timescale.

- Goals are relevant and related to a strong underlying reason why. Aims often tend to be based on wishful thinking.

- Goals have timescales to measure what will be achieved by a specific date. Aims often have vague timescales or none at all.

- Goals are worthwhile to the individual.

- Goals are based on personal performance rather than comparative achievements of others.

- Goals only contain what (not how or why) the difference will be.

- Goals only contain one measurable difference.

- Goals are only defined for what the individual can influence and is prepared to be accountable for.

- Goals must be in harmony with other goals that the person has defined.

- Goals can relate to having, being, doing or learning.

- Goals can be divided into sub-goals.

- Goals can be defined for short time frames (i.e. less than a minute) in addition to longer term timescales.

- Goals that are written are more likely to be achieved.

- Goals are stated in present tense for maximum impact.

- Goals engage the imagination and utilise the capacity of the sub-conscious mind. (For more information on this subject read chapters 30-35 of The Art of Making A Difference.)

**"Defining big, 'stretch goals' is great.
However, you still need to believe they are achievable."
Ian Chakravorty**

---

38. Differentiating between umbrella goals and SMART goals

When coaching people to make a difference, I have discovered that many initially struggle to convert their vision into a SMART goal. This is not surprising, as the big picture needs to be broken into smaller chunks. Here is an easy way to do that.

1. Umbrella vision / Aim / Big picture

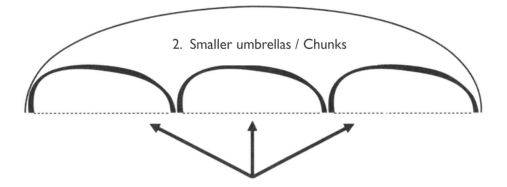

2. Smaller umbrellas / Chunks

3. Worthwhile SMART performance goals (the achievement of which will contribute to the aim or bigger picture)

4. Each SMART goal can be divided into priorities (sub-goals)

5. Each sub-goal can be divided into short-term tasks/actions

If an individual has an aspirational aim or vision and is starting to describe this – often in a non-specific, non-measurable way – then let them. Invite them to label this as the umbrella vision and give it a name. Then help them to identify the components of this vision or break it into smaller chunks. At this point, I am usually drawing a diagram, similar to the one on the previous page, and adding words that the individual says. (Note: this is one of the very few times that I write anything when coaching. Note taking usually focuses on the content and is therefore best left to the individual to take responsibility for. However, in this situation, I am focusing on process and my intention is to use a visual format to help the individual understand.) By continuing this process of breaking down large umbrellas into smaller chunks, we will soon arrive at a level where the individual feels confident that they can influence and take personal responsibility for making a difference.

39. Case study example – umbrella goal

The following example is an extract from a demonstration coaching session that Ian conducted as part of a training programme. He invited a participant to share with the group an umbrella vision or non-measurable aspirational difference he wanted to make.

Ian: "What difference do you want to make?"

Individual: "I'm not sure. I just want to be happier in life."

Ian: "That's a great vision. Let's label that big umbrella 'being happier in life.'" (draws umbrella and labels it) "What are the aspects of life that you want to be happier about?"

Individual: "I guess there are three: financial, work/life balance and family relationships."

Ian: (draws smaller umbrellas) "Those seem like smaller umbrellas. Which one of those is the most important to you at the moment?"

Individual: "A better work/life balance — because that affects everything I do."

Ian: "How strong is your reason for wanting to make a difference in this area?"

Individual: "Extremely, I know that it can't go on for much longer... or else!"

Ian: "So in order for you to make a difference about your work/life balance, what are the areas that you are prepared to do something about?"

Individual: "The main area is the hours that I work. I know that I'm my own worst enemy and I should leave earlier, but I don't."

Ian: "What are the other things that you could achieve that would contribute to a better work/life balance?"

Individual: "Exercising, making better use of my travelling time and planning in time for more social activities."

Ian: (adds labels to diagram) "What else?"

Individual: "No, that's it. Those are the four things that would make it happen."

Ian: "Now, the next step is to be more specific about the tangible differences you want to make. Which one are you most motivated to do something about?"

At this point, Ian went into helping the individual define a SMART goal for one of the four areas he had identified. So, in the process of answering eight H.Q.Q.'s the individual had moved from a vague umbrella aim to focusing on a worthwhile outcome goal. Let's analyse that previous coaching dialogue and Ian will share with you his observations.

Ian: "What difference do you want to make?"

This is an obvious question to start most coaching sessions with. It immediately places the responsibility to choose with the individual.

Individual: "I'm not sure. I just want to be happier in life."

There is some hesitation in answering the question, hence I decide to include a reassurance in my response. I am careful not to get content seduced by asking questions about the meaning of happiness. If I ask a reason why question at this point I might get too much content, so I decide to stick with the vision/goal focus.

Ian: "That's a great vision. Let's label that big umbrella 'being happier in life.'" (draws umbrella and labels it)

"What are the aspects of life that you want to be happier about?"

This question focuses the individual on future success, as does the diagram which I have started to draw.

Individual: "I guess there are three: financial, work/life balance and family relationships."

The individual remains focused on the piece of paper, so I add three smaller umbrellas to the diagram.

Ian: (draws smaller umbrellas) "Those seem like smaller umbrellas. Which one of those is the most important to you at the moment?"

I am inviting the individual to prioritise in order that I can ask future H.Q.Q.'s about this area.

Individual: "A better work/life balance – because that affects everything I do."

Now I decide to test the strength of his reason why.

Ian: "How strong is your reason for wanting to make a difference in this area?"

I await his response and am keen to observe if vocal tone and body language are congruent with the words used in his reply.

Individual: "Extremely, I know that it can't go on for much longer... or else!"

A fast response, with a reflective pause before a powerful end to the statement. I resist the obvious content seduction of enquiring about the meaning of the last two words, but note that the reason why is an away from motivation (i.e. to prevent the "or else" from happening.)

Ian: "So in order for you to make a difference about your work/life balance, what are the areas that you are prepared to do something about?"

Notice that this question contains the presupposition that the individual must be prepared to take personal responsibility in order to make a difference.

Individual: "The main area is the hours that I work. I know that I'm my own worst enemy and I should leave earlier, but I don't."

This response contains a lot of information about beliefs and personal responsibility, which I mentally note. It also implies there are other areas — these need to be identified and labelled.

Ian: "What are the other things that you could achieve that would contribute to a better work/life balance?"

Notice that the question invites the individual to consider things that he believes to be achievable.

Individual: "Exercising, making better use of my travelling time and planning in time for more social activities."

At this point, the individual is actually tapping his finger on the umbrella diagram to indicate where these things should be written. So I add labels to the diagram.

Ian: (adds label to diagram) "What else?"

A simple, but powerful, H.Q.Q. that presupposes that there is always more.

Individual: "No, that's it. Those are the four things that would make it happen."

The individual sits back in his chair, smiling and feeling pleased for figuring it out for himself!

Ian: "Now, the next step is to be more specific about the tangible differences you want to make. Which one are you most motivated to do something about?"

We have now arrived at the level where the individual can define SMART goals. However, first, he needs to take personal responsibility and choose which one. This is the diagram he is now looking at:

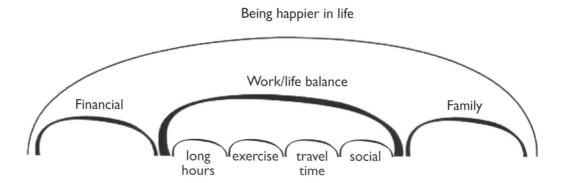

TIME TO REFLECT

Consider the following questions:

What have I realised from studying this case study example?

What do I want to learn more about?

40. Defining SMART goals

TIME TO REFLECT

Spend some time practicing writing a SMART goal for yourself. Think of a difference that you want to make and answer the following questions:

By what exact date will I have made a difference?

Specifically what will that difference be?

How will I measure my success?

How achievable do I believe this to be?

How relevant is this difference to the organisation's objectives or my personal values?

What is my SMART goal (in a single sentence)?

By........./........./.........(date) I will have............................as measured by...........................

Imagine that on the exact date you have stated, an auditor arrives to measure the difference you have made. From reading that one sentence, will the auditor have the necessary specific detail to measure the exact difference? If not, then the goal is not SMART.

Here is an example:

Aim = to write a book.

This is non-specific and without a date. The auditor would ask questions like:

- what is the subject/title of the book?

- in what format will it be written (i.e. handwritten, typed)?

- what evidence will exist (i.e. manuscript, computer file, bound book)?

Goal = By 1st August this year, 5,000 copies of the third edition book "Solution Focused Coaching" will have been printed and bound.

This is a SMART goal that can be audited by either a visit to the printers or the warehouse where the books are stored. The auditor will know specifically the difference to be measured.

Now imagine that the auditor is you, and you have travelled forward in time to measure the evidence of your success. You are about to audit the difference you have successfully made. Here are some questions to consider:

- what will I be able to see, hear, touch, taste or smell?

- what evidence will I have in terms of time, cost, quantity or quality?

- what will exist that currently does not exist?

Here are a few more examples of SMART goals:

By 30th October this year, I will have presented a written proposal relating to project X to the main board of directors.

By 17th December this year members of the customer service team will have undertaken one day of training relating to project X.

By 9th January next year the monthly income from Leisure Services Division will exceed £780,000.

Notice that the goals state what "will" happen, rather than what they "want" to happen. Always convert a percentage increase into the amount that will be achieved by a specific date i.e. keep the focus on what you want. Similarly if defining goals relating to health and fitness, never define goals about losing weight; always focus on the weight you will be by a specific date.

"Why not spend some time determining what is worthwhile for us, and then go after that?"
William Ross

When coaching others to define goals, watch out for and challenge non-specific words. These commonly include: improve; better; more; less; feel; and generally.

41. Defining measurable qualitative goals

When people comment that some things cannot be measured, it means that they have not yet learned how to define qualitative goals. Everything can be measured – if only on an internal self-measurement scale. The most common example that I encounter when coaching is when a person wants to define a goal about developing greater confidence (self-belief) in their ability to do something. So how can confidence be measured?

The answer involves using a three-stage process: an internal assessment measure; establishing either an internal or external benchmark; and then applying a simple gap analysis. The following example illustrates this.

42. Case study example – qualitative goal

Andy: "What specific difference do you want to make?"

Individual: "I want to feel more confident in giving presentations to the senior management team."

Andy: "How confident do you currently feel about doing this? Use your own internal 1-10 feelings scale to assess your confidence."

Individual: "I'm probably a 3 or a 4 at the moment."

Andy: "By what date do you want to have increased your confidence?"

Individual: "30th September of this year, because I have an end of quarter presentation to give on that day."

Andy: "How high on your internal scale would you like to be?"

Individual: "I'd like to be a 10, but I don't think that's achievable in the next two months."

Andy: "What do you believe is achievable within that timescale?"

Individual: "I could definitely get to a 6."

Andy: "And how worthwhile would that be?"

Individual: "Very, but I'm not sure how I will do it."

Andy: "Let's leave the how until later and focus for the moment on defining what you want."

Individual: "Sure."

Andy: "Let me ask you a couple more questions. Have you ever been a 6 before - when giving a presentation?"

Individual: "Yes, but not to this group. I usually give a presentation to less senior people."

Andy: "So you know what a 6 feels like when giving a presentation?"

Individual: "Yes, I suppose I do."

Andy: "Close your eyes for a second and remember a recent example of giving a presentation where you felt confident."

Individual: "Okay."

Andy: "What is your level of confidence?"

Individual: "It's an 8."

Andy: "Notice what an 8 is like... what it feels like... what is sounds like...notice in detail."

Individual: (opening eyes and excited) "That's what I want it to be like with the senior managers – not a 6 – I want it to be an 8."

Andy: "So just let me check the goal you have defined: On the 30th September, my feeling of confidence will be an 8 (on my internal measurement scale) when delivering my end of quarter report to the senior management team."

Individual: "Yes, that's it."

Now that the benchmark was established, the coaching session moved into generating possibilities to fill the gap between the current situation and the defined goal. However, before you move to a different part of the ThinkOn® Results Framework, let's analyse the dialogue of this goal defining activity.

Andy: "What specific difference do you want to make?"

Individual: "I want to feel more confident in giving presentations to the senior management team."
A non-specific response (feel more confident) that indicates a qualitative measurement will be necessary.

Andy: "How confident do you currently feel about doing this? Use your own internal 1-10 feelings scale to assess your confidence."
I described it as a feelings scale to mirror the words that the individual was using.

Individual: "I'm probably a 3 or a 4 at the moment."
I don't need to know what this means on his scale. My role is to cause him to assess himself.

Andy: "By what date do you want to have increased your confidence?"
Identifying the timescale of SMART.

Individual: "30th September of this year, because I have an end of quarter presentation to give on that day."
The reason why is identified.

Andy: "How high on your internal scale would you like to be?"
Seeking to identify the success measure for the goal.

Individual: "I'd like to be a 10, but I don't think that's achievable in the next two months."
A strong reason why indicated by tone of voice, but a low self-belief. Therefore, I need to identify what he does believe to be achievable.

Andy: "What do you believe is achievable within that timescale?"

This question relates to the achievability link between self-belief and define goal in the framework.

Individual: "I could definitely get to a 6."

High self-belief as he emphasises the word "definitely." I decide to question if 6 is high enough to feel he has made a difference.

Andy: "And how worthwhile would that be?"

Individual: "Very, but I'm not sure how I will do it."

I notice he is starting to think about how to make a difference. I need to remain focused on the framework and defining the goal.

Andy: "Let's leave the how until later and focus for the moment on defining what you want."

Individual: "Sure."

Compliance with suggestion, indicates good trust in the coaching process.

Andy: "Let me ask you a couple more questions. Have you ever been a 6 before – when giving a presentation?"

A deliberate closed question to establish if he has an internal benchmark.

Individual: "Yes, but not to this group. I usually give a presentation to less senior people."

A vital clue that his confidence is influenced by the seniority of the people he presents to.

Andy: "So you know what a 6 feels like when giving a presentation?"

A deliberate reminder to make him consciously aware of this.

Individual: "Yes, I suppose I do."

A lengthy pause and specific eye movements indicate an attempt to recall this happening.

Andy: "Close your eyes for a second and remember a recent example of giving a presentation where you felt confident."

The instruction is well received and he closes his eyes.

Individual: "Okay."

Andy: "What is your level of confidence?"

This question is answered after approximately 10-15 seconds of silence, during which the person has his eyes closed.

Individual: "It's an 8."

Andy: "Notice what an 8 is like ... what it feels like ... what it sounds like...notice in detail."

I use deliberate pauses after each instruction to allow time for the individual to gather information. I notice him start to smile as if he is enjoying the memory.

Individual: (opening eyes and excited): "That's what I want it to be like with the senior managers – not a 6 – I want it to be an 8."

He has now defined the difference he wants to make. There is no need to check how achievable this is as previously he had stated that he could definitely achieve a 6.

Andy: "So just let me check the goal you have defined: On the 30th September, my feeling of confidence will be an 8 (on my internal measurement scale) when delivering my end of quarter report to the senior management team."

I always summarise the defined goal, before moving onto the next part of the framework, to confirm that this is the difference the individual wants to make.

Individual: "Yes, that's it."

Note: There are several ways of helping an individual to benchmark their qualitative goal and it is important that this happens. If the individual does not have an internal or external reference point for success they will be unable to measure the difference they make. Here are the four main methods I use, in order of effectiveness:

1. an internal reference point based on successful past experience of the actual situation.

2. an internal reference point based on successful past experience of a similar situation (e.g. as in the previous case study) or relatable context.

3. an internal reference point based on imagining a future successful experience of the actual situation.

4. an external reference point based on identifying the behaviours of a successful role model in the actual situation.

TIME TO REFLECT

Consider the following questions:

What have I realised from studying this case study example?

What have I learned about helping others to define SMART qualitative goals?

What am I discovering about coaching using the ThinkOn® Results Framework?

43. Visioning – using imagination to define sensory specific goals

I will start this chapter with a couple of examples to illustrate the difference between ordinary SMART goals and sensory specific goals.

Aim: To go on a safari holiday with my wife.

SMART goal: By 1st January next year I will have been on a Kenyan safari holiday with my wife.

Sensory specific goal: the date is August 23rd and I am sitting in the back of a four-wheel drive safari jeep travelling across the plains of Africa searching for a herd of elephants. My wife is on my left-hand side and I am looking through my binoculars. I can hear the call of several birds above the sound of the tyres bouncing across the dirt track. I feel the sun on my arms and legs, and taste the dust as we accelerate. Somebody shouts and I spot a lion in the undergrowth eating the remains of a recent kill. I hold my wife's hand and think to myself, "this is brilliant!"

"Your success as a coach is in being able to facilitate passionate dreams that truly are within the reach of your clients."
Frederic M. Hudson PhD

All goals are based in the future; the future only exists in our imagination. A key skill in coaching is to ask H.Q.Q.'s that engage the imagination. If people can imagine fear and failure, then they can also be helped to imagine success by changing their focus.

Sensory specific goals engage the senses and are described, as a vision, in present tense, i.e. as if they are actually happening. In essence, they make a SMART goal even more specific by describing the tiny detail. The easiest way to convert a SMART goal to a sensory specific goal is to complete the blanks in the following phrases:

"The date is... and I am... (evidence of success).
I am seeing...
I am hearing...
I am holding/touching...
I am tasting...
I am smelling...
I am feeling...
I am saying/thinking..."

The goal must have more power than any current self-limiting beliefs. Defining sensory specific goals will enable the conscious mind to imprint the desired difference on the subconscious mind. The more vivid, the better.

> "Formulate and stamp indelibly on your mind a
> mental picture of yourself as succeeding.
> Hold this picture tenaciously. Never permit it to fade.
> Your mind will seek to develop this picture."
> **Norman Vincent Peale**

Helping an individual to visualise and imagine success can sometimes increase their reason for wanting to make a difference. Most ordinary SMART goals are quite clinical and matter of fact – good for the auditor, but they don't engage the imagination or emotion of the person seeking to make a difference.

If an individual struggles with defining a sensory specific goal it might reveal that they don't believe it is achievable, and hence they cannot imagine themselves being successful. It is considerably easier to state, "I will have made a difference by a specific date" than to imagine it happening. Hence, as a coach, it is useful to use sensory specific goals to check people's motivation and self-belief.

> "I dream for a living."
> **Steven Spielberg**

44. High quality questions to ask

Both types of H.Q.Q.'s can be asked to help an individual define a goal. H.Q.Q.'s that focus the mind are useful to help the person to become more sensory specific by imagining successful outcomes. Here are a selection of questions to choose from and add to:

- what difference do you want to make?

- what specifically do you want to achieve?

- what is your measure of success?

- how will you measure your success in terms of time, cost, quantity or quality?

- what is your specific, measurable goal in a single sentence?

- how will you know when you have achieved it?

- by what exact date will you have achieved your goal?

- what specifically do you want to achieve by the end of this coaching session?

- what will you use as evidence to know you have accomplished your goal?

- to what extent do you control the achievement of this goal?

- are you prepared to be held personally responsible for the achievement of this goal?

- what specifically do you want to change?

- what specifically do you want to improve?

- how auditable is your goal?

- what is your target date?

- what evidence will there be of the difference you have made?

- what evidence do you imagine there could be?

- how could you rewrite the goal to make it more motivating for you?

- what other ways are there of measuring your success?

- how achievable is this goal, on a scale of 1-10?

- what do you need to change to make it more achievable?

- how clear is your vision? (describe it.)

- imagine that you have arrived at that future date and you have successfully made a difference. Now, notice:
    - what does it look like?
    - what are you able to see?
    - what does it sound like?
    - what are you able to hear?
    - what does it feel like?
    - what are you saying to yourself?

- what are you able to taste, smell or touch?

- what exists that previously did not exist?

- what difference have you made?

- what difference will other people notice when this goal is achieved?

- how achievable is this difference?

- how relevant is this goal to what's important to you?

- how relevant is this goal to what's important to your organisation?

- what is the relevance of this goal?

- whose goal is this – yours or someone else's?

- by when do you want to have chosen what goal to define? (in response to the individual not knowing what they want i.e. this is defining a goal about defining a future goal.)

- what steps can you take to define your goal more precisely?

- what are the tangible components of your umbrella vision?

- what are the smaller chunks of this big picture that can be specifically measured?

- how can you convert this wonderful vision into achievable goals?

- if you were audited on that exact date, what evidence would an auditor have?

- what specific difference will have been made that currently does not exist?

- if I was to visit you on that date, what would I notice that is different?

- how relevant is your goal to organisational priorities?

- how does this goal link back to your reason why?

- how can you phrase that in terms of what you do want? (in response to the individual stating what they don't want.)

- if you don't want that, what is it you do want?

- what will be the difference on your internal 1-10 scale?

And finally, before moving on to the next stage of the framework, a useful summary question:

— what is your defined SMART goal in a single sentence?

Remember that I am deliberately providing you with more questions than you will ever need. So pick the ones you like or highlight the ones you want to refer back to.

45. Linking the defined goal with other ThinkOn® Key Principles

The second ThinkOn® Key Principle links with five others in the framework.

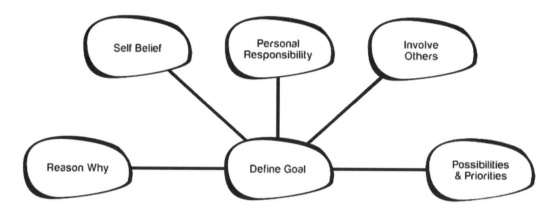

The diagram on the next page illustrates which order these links are most naturally followed during the coaching session. Notice that there are several options.

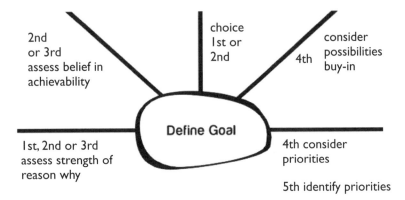

A ThinkOn® coaching session always starts with either identifying a strong reason why or defining the goal. It does not matter which comes first. If the individual chooses to accept responsibility for defining a goal with the help of a coach, then there is no need for the coach to ask any questions about this link as it is automatically made in the process of goal defining.

The strength of the reason why might already have been assessed before the goal is defined. Alternatively this link might be made whilst defining the goal or immediately afterwards.

The achievability line is questioned as part of the SMART process and could therefore be assessed before the strength of the reason why is identified. I normally only ask one question at this point (usually involving a 1-10 scale) to identify if the person's self-belief is stronger than their self-doubt that the goal will be achieved.

"Whatever the mind can conceive and believe,
It can achieve."
Napoleon Hill

Once a SMART goal has been defined, the strength line must be checked, if this has not already happened. Once the why and the what have been completed, then, and only then, is it time to move onto the how. The start of the how process is the first of the three P's – possibilities. One area of possibilities is the buy-in line, and the next section of the framework will highlight the possible need to involve others in defining the goal in order to obtain their buy-in.

Only after the process of generating possibilities has been completed should priorities be identified. This involves linking back to the defined goal to determine which of the possibilities is most important.

46. What to watch out for: defining goals

During coaching the defined goal might change or need to be redefined for several reasons:

- the individual's self-belief might change and hence the timescale or measurement of difference might need to increase or decrease.

- another difference might be identified that has a stronger underlying reason why.

- the reason why might not be sufficiently strong.

- another goal might be identified through SMARTening a priority.

- a realisation, by the individual, that others need to be involved in defining the difference to be made.

- the goal needs to be broken down into smaller pieces (sub-goals) in order to develop an action plan.

- the individual does not want to be accountable and take personal responsibility for the achievement of the goal.

If the individual is unwilling or reluctant to define a goal it is likely that they are not prepared to take personal responsibility for making a difference because either their self-belief or reason why is not strong enough.

> "Since I was twenty-four, there never was any
> vagueness in my plans or ideas as to what
> God's work was for me."
> **Florence Nightingale**

Here are some more things to watch out for when helping others define goals, together with some tips on handling certain situations:

- Goals that need to be divided because they contain two or more outcomes. It is more satisfying for an individual to achieve separate successes.

- The person wants to tell you in detail about the background situation before defining the goal. Tip: explain that in your role as coach you don't need to know the detail (content) and then focus on the process of goal defining.

- Tip: carefully observe the person's body language, particularly their facial expressions, when defining goals. You can gain many clues about their level of self-belief, especially when converting a SMART goal into a sensory specific goal.

- Individuals who focus on what they don't want. Tip: this is a good indication of away motivation (reason why). It can often be useful to invite them to imagine a future difference in order to focus their attention away from current reality.

- Individuals who want to define many goals at the same time. Tips: ask them to prioritise and choose the most important to focus on. Notice if any of the goals are related and there is a possible logical order i.e. one is a sub-goal of another and has to be achieved in order for a larger goal to be achieved.

- Tip: invite the person being coached to write down their goal during the coaching session.

– Tip: use your imagination to create short exercises designed to stretch the imagination of the person defining the goal. For example, "Imagine writing a speech to be given on the date you will successfully make a difference. What would it contain? What would be your achievements?" (Note: the answer to these questions can either be said out loud to the coach or imagined internally by the individual.)

"If I think I can't have it,
I imagine myself with it,
And then I go out and get it."
Nadine Taylor

– Tip: as a coach, set yourself goals and milestones to achieve when coaching others. This will increase your self-belief and make you feel good when you achieve them.

SECTION THREE

47. Generating possibilities – 10 common areas

Finally, we are onto the *how* part of the ThinkOn® system. The good news is that this is the easy part – if the *why* and the *what* have already been sorted out!

The first stage of the how part involves generating possibilities. The role of the coach is to help the individual identify as many possibilities as time permits. This involves the use of H.Q.Q.'s to engage the imagination, think creatively, consider options and implications, challenge limited thinking and stretch beyond what the individual had previously thought. The emphasis is on the quantity and variety of possibilities – not the quality of them. The greater the number of possibilities, the greater the flexibility in making choices.

"Here is Edward Bear, coming downstairs now,
bump, bump, bump on the back of his head,
behind Christopher Robin.
It is, as far as he knows,
the only way of coming downstairs,
but sometimes he feels that there really is another way,
if only he could stop bumping for a moment
and think of it."
Winnie the Pooh

Generating possibilities encompasses two key principles and two link lines within the ThinkOn® Results Framework. The arrows indicate movement backwards and forwards between these key principles in order to generate a high number of possibilities.

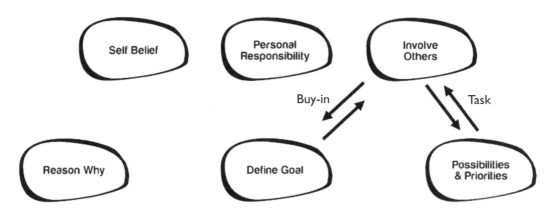

When using ThinkOn® as a coaching framework there are ten areas for which possibilities are commonly generated. From looking at the previous diagram, it is easy to identify three of these:

1. possible tasks and things to do

2. possible others to involve

3. possible ways to gain buy-in

"In the beginner's mind there are many possibilities:
In the expert's mind there are few."
Shunryu Suzuki

Here is the full list of the ten ThinkOn® possibility thinking areas which can be generically applied to any subject area:

1. possible tasks

2. possible resources

3. possible reasons to involve others

4. possible others to involve

5. possible ways to communicate the goal to others

6. possible ways to obtain buy-in

7. possible obstacles

8. possible risks and implications

9. possible ways to overcome obstacles and reduce risks

10. possible assumptions and self-imposed limitations

The easiest way to remember these ten areas is to notice that the first two areas are about "things", the next four relate to involving others and the final four relate to issues and things that might prevent the goal from being achieved. It is important to be flexible in the sequence in which H.Q.Q.'s are asked to help the individual think about the areas, rather than clinically working through the list of areas.

Your role, as a coach, is to stimulate the thinking of the individual, getting them to explore and generate a quantity of ideas through asking H.Q.Q.'s designed to engage their imagination.

48. High quality questions to ask

Investing time in this part of the Results Framework is essential. Encouraging individuals to generate possibilities is rewarding for both them and yourself. I spend approximately 50% of each coaching session generating possibilities by asking H.Q.Q.'s about the ten possibility areas. When I am coaching myself for major personal or business goals, I nearly always set myself the sub-goal of generating a minimum of 40 possibilities. Last week when I was coaching a team, they generated 76 possibilities. Of these possibilities, six priorities were identified – one of which was the 67th possibility!

It is okay to repeat questions during this stage of the coaching session and to ask the same question in a slightly different way. Encourage the individual to capture the possibilities by writing them down. Leave silences whilst the person writes and thinks. Observe how fast they write and pick up clues from their body language to guide you when to ask the next question.

Here is a list of H.Q.Q.'s to use, adapt and add to. Remember to highlight the ones you might want to use:

– what possible actions have you already considered?

– what else could you possibly do?

– who else could you possibly involve?

– how else could you possibly do that?

– what possible tasks might need completing?

– what possible things could help you?

– how could others possibly help you?

– what possible help might you need that others could provide?

– who could you possibly involve?

– what could you learn from others that would possibly help you achieve your goal?

– where else could you possibly get information from?

– how else could you gain or involve the expertise you require?

– who could possibly support you?

- what are the possible reasons for involving others?

- what tasks could you possibly delegate?

- what are you possibly taking for granted?

- what have others done that could be of possible use to you?

- what could you do today that might possibly help you to move towards your goal?

- how could you communicate your goal in a way that will influence others?

- what are you prepared to possibly sacrifice?

- what possible factors outside your control might impact on your success?

- what possible obstacles might you face?

- how could you possibly overcome these?

- what are the options?

- what possible contingencies could you plan for?

- what are the possible cost implications?

- what resources might possibly be useful?

- how could you obtain the buy-in of others?

- how could you ensure that their commitment/motivation is maintained?

- what could others possibly contribute?

- who do you need to possibly buy-in to your goal?

- how could you possibly communicate the strength of your reason why?

- what could you possibly do to help them feel special?

- who might be the single greatest help to you?

- who is possibly affected by the pursuit and achievement of your goal?

- what are the possible benefits of involving other people?

- if you could select any person to help you, who would it be?

- what possible skills are required?

- how could you motivate others to become involved?

- what are the possible reasons why others might support you?

- how could you identify where to obtain help?

- what alternatives are there?

- what are the possible implications?

- what are the possible risks in pursuing your goal?

- what possible incentives are there for others to become involved?

- how could you encourage others to support your goal?

- what possible limitations are you placing on your abilities?

- what will others possibly gain from becoming involved?

- who could possibly help you to influence others?

- what else?

- how else?

- who else?

The last three questions are the easiest possibility generating questions to ask and can be repeated many times during the same coaching session.

> "Ideas are like rabbits.
> You get a couple and learn how to handle them,
> and pretty soon you have a dozen."
> John Steinbeck

49. Effective phrasing of possibility questions

It is important to recognise the difference between tenses when asking possibility questions; it is easy to unconsciously slip into asking priority questions. Let me illustrate the difference:

"What *could* you do?"

This question focuses on possibilities, i.e. what the person could possibly do. Whereas the following question focuses on priorities, i.e. what the person will do.

"What *will* you do?"

This question invites the person to decide about definite future actions. It is a choice question based upon the link line between personal responsibility and possibilities & priorities and does not belong in the possibility generation part of the coaching session.

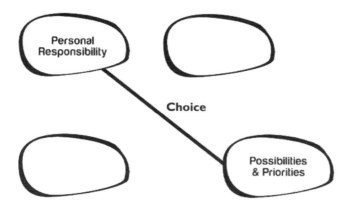

The second common mistake in phraseology is illustrated in the following example:

"What possible actions *have* you thought about?"

"What possible actions *could* you think about?"

The first question might be useful to ask, however it focuses the individual on the past possibilities they have already identified. It is therefore unlikely to generate new ones. The second question focuses on generating new possibilities and is therefore of higher quality.

> "The more I learn, the more I realise
> how much I don't know."
> Albert Einstein

Other common mistakes relating to poor phraseology of possibility questions include:

- using closed questions like, "Anything else?", "Anyone else?" instead of open questions, "What else?", "Who else?" These latter questions invite and expect an answer, whilst the closed questions allow the individual to stop thinking about possibilities.

- giving advice in disguise, e.g. "Don't you think you should consider involving...?" This indicates the coach has got involved in the content instead of remaining focused on the process. A suitable H.Q.Q. would be, "Who else could you consider involving?"

50. Possible reasons to involve others

Here is a list of 28 possible reasons to involve others. These can be used to stimulate your thinking about a personal goal or adapted into questions to coach others:

- to provide useful knowledge or access to it
- to provide specialist skills
- to gain insight from those with experience
- to influence other people
- to provide access to key people
- to enable decisions to be made
- to provide resources
- to save time
- to generate ideas
- to have fun
- to gain credibility

- — to maintain organisational politics

- — to complete tasks

- — to help organise

- — to provide emotional support

- — to provide financial support

- — to bounce ideas off

- — to inspire or build confidence

- — to develop the skills and knowledge of others

- — to learn

- — to gain alternative viewpoints

- — to keep the dream alive

- — to maintain momentum

- — to delegate tasks

- — to reduce their resistance to change

- — to improve action planning

- — to provide feedback

- — to keep focused

"Keep away from people who try to belittle your ambitions. Small people always do that, but the really great make you feel that you, too, can become great."
Mark Twain

51. Think laterally about who to involve

Key Principle five (involving others) is the most lateral thinking part of the ThinkOn® Results Framework. When identifying who can possibly help in making a difference this list could potentially include: people that are known; people that are not known; anyone in the world; anyone who has ever lived; fictional characters; and even imaginary friends!

Now, before you think that I have completely lost the plot, and actually gone mad, allow me to explain further. Most people, when asked about who they could possibly involve in making a difference, naturally focus on those people they know and are most familiar with. For a coach, that is only a starting point! Consider the following question:

"Who do you know, who might know someone who knows someone else who can put you in contact with a person who can introduce you to another person who knows the person with the information that will help you?"

The above question is designed to convey a concept known as the sixth degree of separation. This means that you are only ever six people away from gaining access to a person or the information that you need. Whether this is true, or not, it is not as important as understanding the concept.

"Our aspirations are our possibilities."
Robert Browning

The use of the internet and social media enable the worldwide involvement of others whom we have never met. It is also relatively easy to access written, audio and visual information that has been left by people no longer alive. Reading a book is a simple way of involving others. By reading this book you are already involving Ian and myself in helping you to make a difference!

So, what about fictional characters and imaginary friends? This involves engaging the imagination of the individual to explore possibilities from a third person perspective or experience a different emotional state. An example of this, from a recent training programme, happened when a woman explained how she developed the confidence to sing a solo at a friend's wedding. Her previous experience had been singing in a choir and at the wedding she found it helpful to imagine that she had a friend standing behind her who was also singing. If this perhaps seems a little strange, consider friends or work colleagues who have been inspired by a fictional character in a film or a book.

As a coach, when helping an individual to generate possibilities about who to involve, it is important to think beyond the day-to-day reality. Someone once said that imagination is a wonderful thing.

"What is now proved, was once only imagined."
William Blake

---

52. Gaining buy-in from others

The buy-in line encompasses communication of the goal and influencing others to become involved. The person you are coaching might identify this area as the weakest link in achieving their goal and require coaching on it as a priority sub-goal. Hence, it is useful to consider a few key points and H.Q.Q.'s about gaining buy-in.

To gain buy-in it is necessary to consider the needs of others:

— what are their motives for action?

— what are their similar or conflicting goals?

— what are their current priorities?

— what is their level of belief likely to be about the achievability of your goal?

— what is their self-belief in their own ability?

— what is their perception of you?

— what does it look, sound and feel like from their perspective?

— how could you express the importance of your goal and the reasons why in the way you speak?

— how could you inspire others?

> "The passionate are the only advocates who always persuade. The simplest man with passion will be more persuasive that the most eloquent without."
> René Descartes

- how could you make others feel important and explain why you would like them to be involved?

- how could you communicate how others will benefit from the goal being achieved?

- what interpersonal skills or personal qualities do you need to develop?

- how could you avoid telling them to become involved?

- how could you demonstrate that you will value their contribution?

- how could you invite their opinions, ideas and suggestions?

- how prepared are you to redefine your goal in order to gain their support?

- what could you do to treat others as you know they would like to be treated?

- how could you share the credit for your success with those who you are seeking to involve?

> "Engaging your imagination will help you picture the future; the imagination of others will help you build the future."
> Graham Proud

53. Possible ways to help others generate possibilities

When coaching a person to make a difference it is common to have several coaching sessions – either face to face or by telephone. It might be appropriate to agree an interim goal of generating further possibilities between sessions. Hence a useful question to ask the individual is, "What are the possible ways of generating further possibilities?"

TIME TO THINK

Now ask yourself the same question and list as many possible ways you can think of generating further possibilities.

-             -

-             -

-             -

-             -

-             -

-             -

-             -

-             -

54. What to watch out for when generating possibilities

The individual might ask you for your ideas and possibilities. This often happens to managers who are coaching members of their team. If this happens, there are a couple of options. My preference is to say that I have a few ideas, but before I share them I would like to encourage the individual to generate a few more. Sometimes I ask the person I am coaching if they would like me to step out of my coaching role to contribute professional expertise or personal ideas. If you do want to contribute ideas to the individual and have not been asked to do so, I advise using a simple four-step process.

1. ask permission first e.g. "I've got a couple of ideas that might be useful, would you like to hear them?" This is a deliberate closed question that is unlikely to be refused.

2. reassure the individual that these ideas are not better than any of the possibilities generated so far – they are just additional possibilities.

3. give your ideas, ensuring that they are given as possibilities and not suggestions.

4. reassure once more that these are only possibilities to be added to the list.

**"We don't see things as they are,
we see things as we are."
Anais Nin**

It is important to resume coaching, after contributing any ideas, by asking further H.Q.Q.'s designed to generate further possibilities. This will ensure that your contribution is sandwiched between their ideas and is not given undue prominence when identifying priorities.

Often a person will identify a priority whilst generating possibilities. That is quite natural. An effective coach will simply encourage the individual to record it for later and then return to generating possibilities.

Occasionally a person is too talkative and wants to tell the coach about every possibility in detail that the coach does not need. Tip: let the individual know that you don't need to know the detail. In some cases it might be necessary for you to revert to "blind coaching" where the individual writes down their possibilities without you knowing what they are.

The importance of separating the generation of possibilities and the identification of priorities is to create distance between the two stages and allow the individual to make more informed choices from a wider range of options. Watch out for the individual eliminating possibilities and starting to prioritise before completing the possibility generation stage of the coaching session.

Sometimes people can resist generating future possibilities. This is likely to be caused by internal obstacles e.g. fear, anxiety, anger, old habits and self-talk (the internal messages they give themselves) or external threats e.g. loss of job, financial difficulty, illness and accidents. The individual consumes their energy dealing with the obstacles or situations because they appear overwhelming. Hence a coach needs to understand resistance and aim to help the person minimise the control that the obstacle or threat exerts, and identify possibilities that might minimise the impact. (Note: it is not the role of the coach to remove the resistance, but to help the individual identify ways of diminishing it.) Don't aim to rescue people or give advice. Instead, remind them of their reason why and their defined goal, and allow them to experience feeling temporarily stuck. Eventually they will take personal responsibility for making the best choice they can about the way forward.

"The block of granite which was an obstacle in the pathway of the weak, becomes a stepping-stone in the pathway of the strong."
Thomas Carlyle

Be prepared to move from generating possibilities to building self-belief at any point if an idea or realisation causes the person to question either their own ability or the achievability of the goal. This causes a break in the classic coaching routeway and the coach needs to move back to working the internal triangle (see chapter 14). Developing increased confidence might need to become a priority sub-goal before the individual can resume generating possibilities relating to the original defined goal.

> "We can easily forgive a child who is afraid of the dark; the real tragedy of life is when adults are afraid of the light."
>
> **Plato**

55. More tips and techniques that work

I have outlined below a variety of tips and techniques that I use in the process of helping others generate possibilities:

– Mindstorming: rewrite the defined goal in the form of a H.Q.Q. and then write twenty answers. This is a useful interim exercise between coaching sessions.

– Bubble diagrams: instead of listing possibilities, draw bubbles containing the ten possibility areas (see chapter 47). Encourage the individual to attach possibilities to each bubble. This works well for people who don't like linear lists.

– Alternative words: if a person is struggling to identify possibilities, use different words e.g. ideas, options or alternatives. Notice which they respond best to.

– "What if..." questions: these are useful in helping people to move away from current blocked thinking and assumptions. For example:

"What if you did know?" (in response to, "I don't know.")

"What if that was an imaginary obstacle?"

"What if you could think of one more possibility, what would it be?"

– Using distance or a third person perspective: this allows the individual to gain a different perspective and become more detached with less emotion. For example:

"Imagine looking down from outerspace and having infinite intelligence about the whole universe. What possibilities could you identify?"

– Ask creative H.Q.Q.'s: design questions to stretch the imagination to the extremes. For example:

"If you had a magic wand, what could you do?"

"What's the most outrageous possibility you can think of?"

"What are five possibilities that might achieve the goal, but get you fired?"

"What would the possibilities be if there were no constraints?"

"You've got to believe that there are always more possibilities. They just haven't been discovered yet. The questions you ask are the vehicle for discovery."
Andy Gilbert

– Reverse logic: invite the person to identify everything that is not a possibility. This is useful with people who naturally evaluate, prioritise and reject at the same time as they generate possibilities.

– Role play: invite the individual to pretend being the world's greatest possibility thinker and adopting that role for an imaginary film. However, the film maker is only interested in what the person looks and sounds like – not the content of what is said. Most importantly, the person must look confident, as if everything they say is fantastic. Encourage the individual to really get into the role and ignore what they are actually saying.

– Give praise and encouragement as more possibilities are generated.

56. A pause to reflect on learning so far

The major part of the ThinkOn® coaching session has now been covered. Before moving onto the remainder, pause to reflect on your learning from the past 24 chapters. Consider the following questions:

What have I discovered about using the ThinkOn® Results Framework to structure a coaching session?

What have I realised about the use of high quality questions?

What ideas and tips have been the most useful?

How would I rate my ability to help people define SMART goals about any difference they wanted to make?

What have I learned about defining other types of goals?

What insight have I gained about helping others to generate possibilities?

What can I use to help coach myself more effectively?

What else have I discovered?

SECTION FOUR

57. Deciding priorities

It is now time to complete the second triangle in the ThinkOn®
Results Framework by determining which of the possibilities are
most important and should, therefore, become priorities.

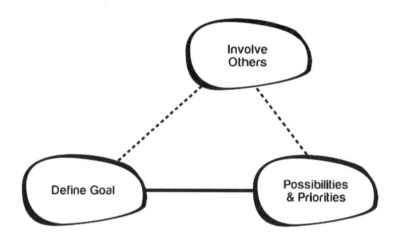

Most people are able to look at their list of possibilities and
within one or two minutes decide what their priorities are. A
few might need some time to reflect and this might be a natural
point to agree a convenient time for a follow-up coaching session.
With complex business situations it might be necessary to involve
others in considering the advantages and disadvantages of various
possibilities, or to conduct a series of cost-benefit analyses to
determine the priorities. This activity, in itself, should be viewed
as a priority sub-goal to be undertaken before resuming coaching
for the overall goal.

"Things that matter most must never be at the
mercy of things that matter least."
Johann Wolfgang von Goethe

It can sometimes be useful to transfer possibilities onto Post-it® notes or other moveable materials that can be rearranged to form clusters. When I am using ThinkOn® as a self-coaching thinking system, I sometimes write my possibilities onto magnetic shapes which I can then manipulate into patterns, from which priorities emerge.

At this stage of the ThinkOn® coaching session, the individual is invited to make conscious choices about what is important, how others will be involved and how much time to allocate to each priority.

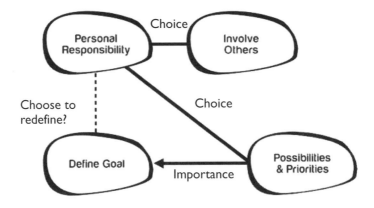

As a consequence of undertaking this prioritisation process, the resulting sub-goals might cause the individual to choose to redefine the original goal.

58. High quality questions to ask

At this stage of the coaching session it is important to ask H.Q.Q.'s that focus the mind on making choices. Here are several to choose from and add to:

− what are your main priorities?

− what do you want to do first?

− what is your criteria for determining priorities?

− what do you see as being the first step?

− which of these possibilities is the most important?

- what is the starting point?

- how will you prioritise your list of possibilities?

- what are your initial priorities?

- how will you prioritise the remainder of your actions?

- what are the necessary actions to take in order to achieve your goal?

- which actions will have the greatest impact?

- what do you need to do immediately?

- which actions are important and urgent?

- what makes it important?

- what is the most important action within your control that will make the greatest difference?

- how will these priorities ensure your goal is achieved?

- what are the most important actions for you to take?

- who will you involve?

- how will you involve them?

- what tasks do you want others to undertake?

- how will you gain their buy-in to your goal?

- how much time do you need to allow?

- what are you prepared to do more of?

- what are you prepared to do less of?

- what is the most important activity on your list of priorities?

- how important is this to achieving your goal?

- how do you know which tasks are more important?

**"The art of being wise is the
art of knowing what to overlook."
William James**

---

59. Defining SMART sub-goals

Once choices have been made and priorities decided, it is time to convert these priorities into SMART sub-goals.

The achievement of these sub-goals will ensure the achievement of the goal. Each sub-goal falls under the umbrella of the original goal.

It is now possible to apply the ThinkOn® system to each sub-goal, if necessary. The following diagrams illustrate how this happens.

Each defined SMART sub-goal is relevant to the original goal. This larger goal now becomes the reason why in the ThinkOn® Results Framework for the existence of the sub-goal.

The framework could continue to be applied to each action if necessary, as these are all differences, albeit smaller, in their own right.

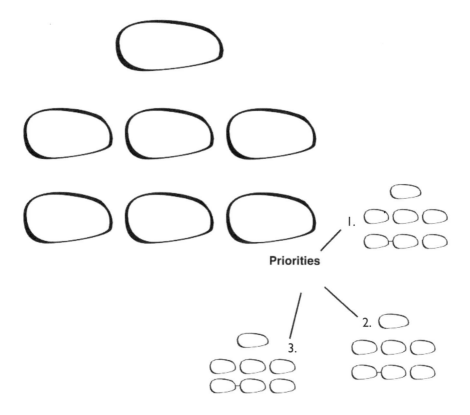

Priorities

1.

2.

3.

SECTION FIVE

60. Building confidence – key points

The fourth ThinkOn® Key Principle relates to developing and maintaining high self-belief. This is a massive specialist subject and there are many excellent books in most major bookshops that can provide further information and build on the information contained in this section. "The Art of Making A Difference" contains 17 chapters and several exercises relating to self-belief and is a good starting point.

As a ThinkOn® coach, one of my aims is to understand how the goal and actions being discussed are impacted by the individual's self-belief. This self-belief is largely comprised of the thoughts, feelings and images that the person has about themselves.

> "Each of us speaks, moves, thinks and feels in a different way, each according to the image of himself that he has built up over the years. In order to change our mode of action, we must change the image of ourselves that we carry within us."
>
> **Moshé Feldenkrais**

In order for individuals to effectively make an external difference it is often necessary for them to make an internal difference for themselves. Quite often, when I am coaching, the focus can shift away from the original goal to an identified sub-goal relating to confidence or self-belief. Hence, as a coach, I often consider whether the coaching should be focused on making an internal or external difference, or both. A good example of this happens quite frequently when coaching people to develop their presentation skills.

Timothy Gallwey in his excellent book, "The Inner Game of Tennis," uses a model for high performance where "potential minus interference is equal to performance." Hence, to increase performance, the interference needs to be reduced or eliminated.(In ThinkOn® coaching this interference includes self-doubt and fear, as well as the absence of defined goals and the evaluation of possibilities at too early a stage.) The role of the coach is to help the individual become aware of how their thoughts, beliefs and self-image affects their perception of reality and ability to make a difference.

"As human beings, our greatness lies not so much in being able to remake the world...as in being able to remake ourselves."
Mahatma Gandhi

Self-belief is largely developed through habit, repetition and past experience which, not surprisingly, influences current thinking and the measurable element of future goals. The five main sources of self-belief are as follows:

— the environment we grew up and live in. This includes our learned models for achievement, success, failure, right and wrong.

— events and experiences in life.

— knowledge, i.e. what has been consciously learned.

— past results, achievements, failures.

— the creation of imagined success through clear goals can increase our self-belief of what is possible.

It is important to remember that people act in accordance with their current beliefs, and these are either limiting or enabling their ability to make a difference.

"Within you right now is the power to do things you never dreamed possible. The power becomes available to you just as you change your beliefs."
Maxwell Maltz

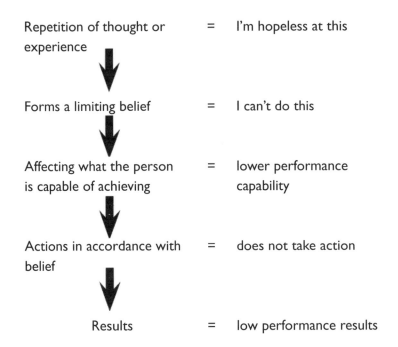

Repetition of thought or experience = I'm hopeless at this

Forms a limiting belief = I can't do this

Affecting what the person is capable of achieving = lower performance capability

Actions in accordance with belief = does not take action

Results = low performance results

61. Linking self-belief with the other ThinkOn® Key Principles

There are three links with self-belief in the ThinkOn® Results Framework.

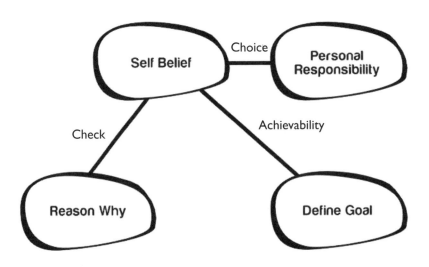

The achievability link has already been explained in chapter 45. A H.Q.Q. is asked early in the coaching session, when defining the goal, to assess the current level of self-belief in its achievability. Once priorities have been identified and converted into SMART sub-goals, the achievability of the overall goal should be assessed once more. If the level of self-doubt is greater than the self-belief then it becomes high priority for the coach to do something about it.

The most common way to increase the self-belief is to redefine the goal by adjusting either the timescale or reducing the measurement of what will be achieved. However, if the coach or individual identifies the cause of low self-belief to be related to one of the sources outlined in the previous chapter, the individual now has a choice. Is the person prepared to develop themself? In a supportive way, an effective coach will challenge the individual to take personal responsibility for their own development. If the individual chooses to do so, the coaching emphasis can change to helping the person make a difference about their self-belief. This is likely to involve defining a qualitative goal as outlined in the case study (chapter 42).

"Come to the edge, he said. They said: we are afraid.
Come to the edge, he said. They came.
He pushed them and they flew."
Guillaume Apollinaire

The final link is with the reason why. This check line is usually completed by asking one or two questions towards the end of the coaching session. It is important for the coach to ensure that the individual still has sufficient self-belief and a strong reason why they want to make a difference.

62. High quality questions to ask

When using ThinkOn® as a coaching framework it is important to remember that the self-belief of the individual is likely to change and possibly fluctuate during the coaching. An effective coach will pay attention to the body language, vocal tone and words spoken by the individual, in order to detect evidence of helpful or hindering thoughts. It might be appropriate to ask H.Q.Q.'s relating to self-belief during the stage of generating possibilities as one of the ten possibility areas relates to possible assumptions and self-imposed limitations.

Here is a list of H.Q.Q.'s to consider. Highlight the ones you might want to use or adapt:

- how achievable on a scale of 1-10 do you believe this goal to be?

- how could you increase this to a higher level?

- how confident are you in your abilities?

- what past experience could you draw on to develop your confidence?

- how could you ensure that you maintain your level of self-belief?

- how capable are you of achieving this goal? (1-10 scale)

- what additional knowledge, skills or experience do you believe you need to develop?

- what could you do to develop greater self-belief?

- what messages (self-talk) do you give yourself?

- what could you say to yourself in order to replace a hindering message with a more helpful one?

- what potential obstacles are you likely to encounter?

- what responsibility are you taking for developing yourself?

- what will be your greatest challenge in making a difference?

- what is your probability of success?

- what affirmations will you use to increase/maintain your self-confidence?

- how could you change that limiting belief?

- in what ways do you limit yourself?

- what would you like to believe about yourself?

- what is your strategy for dealing with any possible setbacks/challenges?

- what concerns do you have?

- what is causing you to feel/react this way?

- how successful do you believe you will be in doing this?

- what makes you so sure?

- are you prepared to develop yourself?

- do you want to take personal responsibility for creating your future, or would you prefer to allow your past beliefs and habits constrain your success? You choose!

Note: this final question is included as an example to illustrate how sometimes it is necessary to challenge people to make choices in order for them to move forward.

"One's philosophy is not best expressed in words;
it is expressed in the choices one makes.
In the long run, we shape our lives
and we shape ourselves.
The process never ends until we die.
And the choices we make
are ultimately our responsibility."
Eleanor Roosevelt

---

63. What to watch out for: self-belief

Throughout the coaching session I am constantly on the lookout for clues that provide possible evidence of low, high, increasing or diminishing self-belief.

1. Common evidence of low or diminishing self-belief:
   - goals that are too easily achievable – perhaps based on past experience
   - constant references to past events/efforts that have been unsuccessful
   - talking about failure and non-helpful images
   - use of "victim language" e.g.
       - "there's nothing I can do."
       - "I can't..."
       - "I have to..."
       - "I know I should, but..."
   - hindering self-belief statements. e.g.
       - "I'm not very good at..."
       - "I'll never be able to..."
       - "I'm too old to..."
   - hesitancy in responses
   - uncertainty language. e.g.
       - "I'm not sure about..."
       - "It might be possible..."
       - "I'll try to..."
   - vocal tone that is incongruent with the words spoken
   - body language, especially facial expressions and reduced eye contact (in Western cultures).

2. Common evidence of high or increasing self-belief:
   - making connections between possibilities to define priorities
   - quick responses to questions
   - emphatic hand gestures e.g. clapping and rubbing hands together
   - excited vocal tone and animated facial expressions
   - increased smiling and self-composure
   - intense, quick responses to questions using a 1-10 assessment scale
   - helpful belief statements, e.g.
       - "I can see how to do it."
       - "I'm certain I can do it."

Evidence of low or diminishing self-belief needs to be immediately addressed by the coach. This is most usually done through the use of H.Q.Q.'s or challenging statements that are made in order to increase the person's ability to make a difference. I often ask myself the question, "What does the individual have to believe to be true in order to say that, do that or think in that way?" I then ask H.Q.Q.'s to check my assumptions.

"All your life you are told things you cannot do.
All your life they will say you're not good enough
or strong enough or talented enough.
They'll say you're the wrong height or the wrong
weight or the wrong type to play this or achieve this.
THEY WILL TELL YOU NO, a thousand times no,
until all the no's become meaningless. All your life they
will tell you no, quite firmly and very quickly.
They will tell you no. AND YOU WILL TELL THEM YES."
Nike advertisement

Give encouragement when you notice enabling beliefs, increasing self-belief and breakthroughs in thinking, e.g. "It's good that you've realised that," "It's great that you've got that confidence."

Be careful about transferring your perceptions of reality (beliefs) onto the individual. Stay focused on asking H.Q.Q.'s to help the person think and avoid getting seduced by the content.

64. Ways to maintain or increase self-belief

The ThinkOn® Results Framework should be viewed by coaches as a framework to create a successful coaching structure. I encourage you to build upon this with whatever knowledge, skills and experience you possess, to help others increase their confidence and self-belief.

The following list is provided as a stimulus for you to add to, develop and help others to apply. These are the twenty things that I consciously do to maintain and develop my self-belief:

- regularly celebrating small successes and the achievement of sub-goals.

- associating with people who are positive; mixing less with those who are negative.

- identifying and meeting role models who have achieved what I want to achieve.

- defining worthwhile sensory specific goals.

- visualising my goals being successfully achieved.

- using positive affirmation statements.

- avoiding unhealthy comparisons and focusing on what is worthwhile to me.

- reading positive, development books.

- being decisive (indecision leads to doubt, which leads to fear).

- eliminating worries by defining them and generating solutions.

- recreating in my mind past experiences of success.

- learning to like myself even more.

- changing any negative mental images into positive ones.

- identifying limiting beliefs and working towards replacing them with enabling beliefs.

- being aware of the messages I give myself.

- replacing hindering self-talk with helpful self-talk.

- reminding myself of current achievements.

- recognising my strengths, abilities and personal qualities.

- identifying sources of enjoyment and positive energy.

- focusing on the differences I want to make and regularly reviewing them.

"Set yourself free from anything that may hinder you in becoming the person you want to be. Free yourself from the uncertainties about your abilities or the worth of your dreams, from the fears that you may not be able to achieve them or that they won't be what you wanted. Set yourself free from the past. The good things from yesterday are still yours in memory; the things you want to forget you will, for tomorrow is only a sunrise away. Free yourself from regret or guilt, and promise to live this day as fully as you can. Set yourself free from the expectations of others, and never feel guilty or embarrassed if you do not live up to their standards. You are most important to yourself; live by what you feel is best and right for you. Others will come to respect your integrity and honesty. Set yourself free to simply be yourself, and you will soar higher than you've ever dreamed."

Edmund O'Neill

SECTION SIX

65. Planning in time to take action

Attention has so far been given to each of the 11 critical links between the first six ThinkOn® Key Principles. The framework is now virtually complete. All that remains is to revisit the choice line between principles three and six and invite the individual to consider how to plan in sufficient time to ensure the SMART sub-goals are achieved.

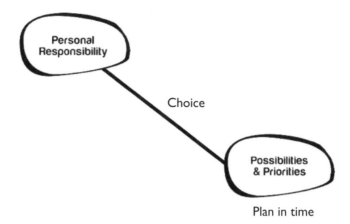

Choice

Plan in time

Watch out for individuals who do not have an effective diary/planning system. They are unlikely to be as effective as those that do. Here are a few H.Q.Q.'s that could be used at this stage:

- what is the most effective way of planning in sufficient time to achieve your goal?

- how much time have you already allowed to undertake these priority tasks?

- how much time do you need to allocate to ensure each sub-goal is achieved?

- how often will you monitor progress and measure results?

- how will you remember to do this?

- when will you do this planning?

- how much time will you set aside for each priority?

- how can you ensure that these will remain a priority in your diary?

> "Time is the one commodity above all others that is our
> true possession...Time's most important quality is
> that it passes, that we have only a finite amount
> of it. Therefore, be aware of its value and know that
> when you give it, share it, or waste it, you are spending
> the most precious commodity that you possess.
> When we give our time, we are giving of our life."
> Daphne Rose Kingma

SECTION SEVEN

66. Testing commitment and personal responsibility

The sixth ThinkOn® Key Principle of taking personal responsibility contains within it the elements of being accountable for the difference (without blaming others) you want to make, being a role model for others and making choices.

Telling a person that they are personally responsible does not make them accept accountability. As a ThinkOn® coach it is important to watch for signs that the person is taking personal responsibility. The evidence of this will mainly be the response given to H.Q.Q.'s designed to focus the mind.

> "If you wish to know your past life look to your present
> circumstances. If you wish to know your
> future life look to your present actions."
> Buddhist saying

67. High quality questions to ask

I sometimes describe the final few coaching questions as "ultimate" H.Q.Q.'s. Several of these are deliberately closed questions to focus the individual on choosing whether or not to take personal responsibility. Listed on the next page are a few H.Q.Q.'s to consider using:

- are you prepared to take personal responsibility for achieving this goal?

- are you prepared to be held accountable for making this difference?

- how will you demonstrate your accountability?

- how certain are you that you will do what you say you are going to do? (1-10 scale)

- how will you act as a role model to inspire others?

- what responsibility are you taking for your personal development?

- what decisions do you need to make?

- how will you demonstrate your commitment to making this happen?

- what are you prepared to sacrifice?

- how will you encourage others to follow your example?

- what excuses might you be tempted to make?

- who will you be accountable to?

- what do you choose to do?

- what will you do to maintain your momentum?

> "In times of change learners inherit the Earth, while the learned find themselves beautifully equipped to deal with a world that no longer exists."
> Eric Hoffer

68. Linking personal responsibility with the other ThinkOn® Key Principles

I have previously explained the five choice lines which link the sixth ThinkOn® Key Principle to the previous five. It is now worthwhile to consider the order these choices are most naturally made during the ThinkOn® coaching session.

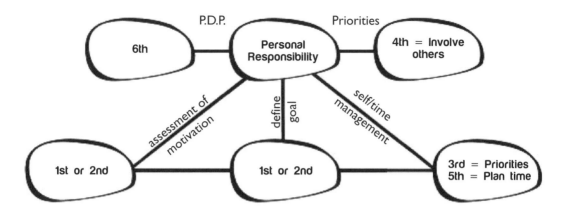

The links with principles one and two are made automatically through the coaching session, i.e. the individual choosing to answer questions to assess the strength of motivation and define a clear goal. The subsequent three link lines require H.Q.Q.'s.

The link with principle three (Possibilities & Priorities) highlights two choices that need to be made – choosing priorities and choosing to plan time. Between choices three and five, is the fourth choice of prioritising who to involve, how to involve them and how to obtain their commitment. Choices three and four tend to happen simultaneously in the prioritising stage of the process.

The link with principle four (self-belief) could happen at any stage of the coaching if the individual chooses to take responsibility for defining a personal development goal. If this does not occur, the person still has a choice at the end of the coaching session.

"I am still learning."
Michelangelo

69. What to watch out for: personal responsibility

Very often, by this stage of the coaching session, I have gained enough evidence that the individual will take personal responsibility and go on to take action. However, occasionally I still need to be convinced, particularly if the person appears to be avoiding making choices. This is normally apparent when I am asking H.Q.Q.'s to test commitment and receiving possibility responses. For example:

Andy: "What specific action will you take?"

Individual: "Well I could do several things."

Andy: "What are you prepared to take personal responsibility for doing?"

Individual: "Yes, I'm thinking about that and I'm not sure."

Andy (still in rapport): "I just want to check out that you're not just talking about making a difference and are actually going to make it happen."

Individual: "Oh yes, I am – definitely."

Andy (challenging): "Convince me that you're serious."

When challenging people to take personal responsibility it is important to maintain good rapport with them to avoid being perceived as aggressive. There will always be an underlying reason why people resist taking decisions and the coach should seek to help the individual become aware of that.

Individual: "I am serious, it's just that... I think I need to involve a few more people to help me."

"All uncertainty is fruitful – so long as it is accompanied by the wish to understand."
Antonio Machado

---

70. A couple of tips

Whenever I am coaching I always have a notepad handy. This is not for me to make notes (unless I am drawing an umbrella goal), but for the individual to do so. At an appropriate point – either when defining the goal or generating possibilities – I hand the notepad over. Accepting it and writing their ideas is an indication of taking personal responsibility.

Towards the end of the coaching session, when I invite people to take responsibility for planning in time, I sometimes issue a challenge for them to get their diary out, allocate time to undertake the sub-goals and plan in review dates to measure the results. Once again, I am deliberately testing their commitment to making a difference.

Another technique, that I use at this point, is to invite the person to use their imagination to visualise their future actions in detail and mentally rehearse being successful. Their ability and willingness to do this is a measure of their level of commitment. Mental rehearsal is also a useful self-belief building technique.

"What one does is what counts and not what one had the intentions of doing."
Pablo Picasso

71. The final questions – celebrating success

"How will you celebrate success?"

"How will you involve others who have helped you?"

These are nice questions to end a coaching session with, as they engage the imagination and focus the individual on future success.

SECTION EIGHT

72. Agreeing the way forward

I am often asked on our development programmes, "How do I end a coaching session?" I tend to respond with, "It depends how you started it!"

Establishing clear ground rules at the start of a coaching relationship will help both the coach and the person being coached to share an understanding of what will happen during and after the coaching session. These ground rules typically include frequency and length of coaching support, the role of the coach and the responsibility of the individual.

I tend to end most of my one to one coaching sessions with a deliberate closed question, e.g. "Is there anything more I can help you with in this session?" You will know to finish a coaching session when it feels right – usually when the individual has planned their commitment to take action. Oh yes, and most people will usually thank you for helping them.

Once you have been through the framework, helped the individual to apply the key principles and checked the links through H.Q.Q.'s you will definitely have further developed that person's ability to make a difference.

"We make a living by what we get,
but we make a life by what we give."
Winston Churchill

73. Reviewing progress

The seventh ThinkOn® Key Principle is Taking Action and Measuring Results. Whilst this is the responsibility of the individual, depending on the nature of your coaching relationship, it might be appropriate to arrange a progress review coaching session for a future date. Listed below are a few more H.Q.Q.'s that might prove useful during a progress review:

- what measurable differences have been made?
- how have you progressed towards achieving your goal?
- how successful have you been?
- what lessons have you learned?
- how have you measured your progress?
- what do you need to do more or less of?
- who else do you need to involve?
- what other possibilities do you need to consider?
- how achievable do you believe your goal to be?
- what is your next priority?
- how have you celebrated your success so far?
- how strongly motivated are you to continue?
- what is the next step you are committed to taking?

> "My strength lies solely in my tenacity."
> Louis Pasteur

74. A pause to reflect on learning so far

That's it – or very nearly! Most of what I know and apply as a ThinkOn® coach has already been written in this book, and as someone once said, "All good things must come to an end." Well, at least, I hope you have found it good! Do you remember at the beginning of this book, I challenged you to write in it? Have you? Are you serious about making a difference or have I been wasting my time? (Only joking!)

TIME TO REFLECT

Consider what you have read so far. Reflect on your understanding and realisations as you contemplate the following questions:

What has been the most significant realisation I have had about making a difference?

How can I use this when coaching myself and others?

What have I discovered about applying ThinkOn® as a coaching framework?

What have I learned about coaching?

How confident am I in my ability to coach using the ThinkOn® Results Framework?

What could I do to increase my confidence and ability?

What do I want to do as a result of reading this book?

PART FOUR: TIPS, TECHNIQUES AND SITUATIONS

This section contains a collection of coaching tips and techniques that I have picked up over the past twenty years. Many of them were learned before ThinkOn® was researched and applied as a coaching framework. I have to admit that I was tempted to leave this section out. However, in the end I was seduced by the content, as I believe that most people will be able to find at least a couple of tips to help them become even more excellent at coaching.

Rather than write lengthy explanations, which would more than double the size of this book, I have focused on providing you with bullet point insights. If you want more, then you will have to take personal responsibility.

75. More tips about coaching

- Remember that coaching isn't always comfortable for the individual being challenged by H.Q.Q.'s.
- Avoid content seduction when coaching by using the "suitcasing" technique of packing your thoughts, ideas and experiences into an imaginary suitcase.
- Relax when you don't make a difference – seek to understand the cause and learn from your understanding.
- Understand that you are not perfect and will make mistakes.
- Adapt your style and vocal tone to suit each person you coach.
- "Invite" a person to consider something, rather than tell them.
- Give yourself some positive self-talk when coaching others.
- Define goals for yourself when coaching others and mentally celebrate your success.
- Question whether your thoughts are helping or hindering you as a coach.
- Attend a coaching skills training programme.

> **"You become good at coaching by doing it –**
> **not by reading books!"**
> **Andy Gilbert**

– Question your intentions/actions as a coach, i.e. what caused you to ask that question or challenge that comment?

– Remember that every question should have a purpose.

– Practise coaching people to make a difference on an informal basis during conversations by asking H.Q.Q.'s. (They don't have to know you are using coaching skills.)

– Take a break from coaching and give the individual some "homework" by inviting them to consider their answers to 3 or 4 H.Q.Q.'s.

– Invite individuals to take personal responsibility by writing their own notes.

– Ask for feedback from the person you are coaching.

– Use metaphors and stories (as well as H.Q.Q.'s) to engage the imagination.

– Role model using ThinkOn® as a framework by applying to yourself what you have read in this book.

– Remember that coaching can be a series of short, regular sessions.

– Put this book down and practise, practise, practise.

– Learn to spot "coachable moments."

– Offer to coach someone and tell them you want to practise your skills.

– Remember that the impact of your coaching can be more powerful than you give yourself credit for.

– Smile when you receive praise for coaching skills.

– Have fun. Coaching should be enjoyed!

"A candle loses nothing by lighting another candle."
James Keller

---

76. Self-coaching tips

– Use the example H.Q.Q.'s in this book.

– Notice which questions you prefer not to answer.

– Pay attention to the tone of voice you use with yourself.

– Notice when it doesn't work and do something else instead!

77. Coaching the opposite sex

– Watch out for individuals experiencing and reacting to situations differently based on their gender.

– Read some books about the way men and women behave differently.

– Balance the need for awareness of gender issues with the need to keep an open mind.

78. Developing a state of relaxed concentration

– Focus your attention on the individual.

– Relax and let go of thoughts about coaching skills, techniques, models and process. Trust that your subconscious has absorbed that information.

– Keep your mind focused on what is happening.

– Keeping the mind in the present calms it.

– Imagine inserting a clean sheet of white paper into your mind at the start of each coaching session.

– Watch the individual and develop a relaxed, effortless fascination with everything they say and do.

– If your mind wanders to yourself, gently bring it back to focus on the individual once more.

- Notice in detail the appearance of the individual (without staring) including their facial muscle tone and wrinkles.

- Observe changes to the person's physical appearance, tone of voice and breathing pattern in response to questions, silence, uncertainty and choices.

"Let the past drift away with the water."
Japanese saying

---

79. Useful knowledge (coaching made more complex!)

Understand issues relating to adult development and life transitions.

There are common work/life balance issues for young adults; those in their twenties, thirties, forty plus; early achievers; and late peakers.

"The Handbook of Coaching" by Frederic M. Hudson, PhD. (New York, 1999 pub. Jossey Bass) contains over 300 coaching references – more than enough to satisfy the ardent theorist.

80. Increasing awareness

An individual can only make a conscious difference about that which he or she is aware of. Hence the role of the coach is to raise that awareness – usually by asking H.Q.Q.'s. There are two types of awareness that the coach should aim to raise. Firstly, the awareness of external factors, i.e. what is going on in the environment around the individual. This includes awareness of possibilities and who to involve. Secondly, an understanding of the internal factors, i.e. what the individual is thinking and feeling. Exploring the strength of the reason why and self-belief contributes to greater self-awareness. The internal and external triangle diagrams in chapter 14 illustrate this.

81. Offering feedback

In helping to raise the self-awareness of an individual, it is sometimes useful to offer feedback during the coaching session. Notice how I said offer rather than give – this is important! As a coach, remember that feedback is just data without judgement, offered with the intent to help the individual develop greater self-awareness. The feedback I most commonly give is based on my observations during the coaching session. Before presenting this feedback I signal to the individual that I would like to change my coaching style. Here is the three-stage process I use:

1. I indicate that I would like to offer some feedback and ask permission to do so.

    e.g. "I have a few observations about things that you have said so far which I believe might help you. Would you like to hear them?"

2. Once permission is gained, I give the feedback based on my observations of what I have heard and seen. This is almost like replaying the video evidence from a closed-circuit television, i.e. without interpretation.

    e.g. "Ten minutes ago you said you were excited about making this difference. You were smiling and leaning forward. Now you are not smiling and have commented that you are not so sure."

3. I ask a question to help the individual reflect. e.g. "what's causing this shift in behaviour?"

Many years ago I was trained to give feedback as if I was a C.C.T.V. camera. I have found this to be helpful when confronting incongruities between body language and words spoken, and when challenging a vocal tone, e.g. "what does xxxx (mimic person's vocal tone) mean?" The important thing to remember is that this must always be done with the intent of helping the individual to develop greater self-awareness.

> "A gift consists not in what is done or given,
> but in the intention of the giver or doer."
> Lucius Annaeus Seneca

82. Giving advice and information

Recognise that this is not coaching, as it requires content expertise! However, you might have the necessary expertise or relevant information and be asked for it by the person you are coaching. It is important to realise that you are being asked to get involved in the content (principle five – involve others) and that it might not be appropriate at that particular moment to become involved. Hence, this needs to be made clear to the individual that for the time being you wish to remain in the coaching role. However, there are always exceptions! If they can obtain your buy-in at that moment – perhaps because you are their manager or your knowledge could save time now – then it's okay to give advice and information. Just remember that you are now no longer in a coaching role!

> "In seeking wisdom thou art wise;
> In imagining that thou hast attained it – thou art a fool."
> The Talmud

83. Coaching during organisational change and restructuring

Much of my former academic work involved researching the impact of "survivor syndrome" – people adversely affected by change who continue to work in the same organisation. Now, I spend a significant proportion of my consulting time working with organisations to develop strategies for managing the people issues related to organisational change and cultural development. This is a large, potentially complex, area and does not belong in a book about making coaching easy! Hence, I recommend reading, "How to Save Time and Money by Managing Organisational Change Effectively" which I wrote as a practical guide to help managers handle people's reaction to organisational change.

However, there are a couple of significant points to bear in mind when coaching individuals who believe they are adversely affected by change:

- When an adverse change happens, people believe they are losing something of value. In the psychology of transition this is referred to as "endings." When people resist making endings they are attempting to hold on to the past, or old ways of doing things. This will obviously mean that they are unlikely to buy-in to the concept of making a difference.

- An effective coach will recognise that the perceived powerlessness of an individual to influence organisational change is likely to impact on their reason why and self-belief about making a difference. In such circumstances, in order to move forward, the individual first needs to let go of the past. Hence, the role of the coach is to help the person make some endings.

"To be wronged is nothing
unless you continue to remember it."
Confucius

- It is important to an individual to understand the difference between the things that can be influenced and those that are a *given*. Whilst a given cannot be changed, the individual can take personal responsibility for choosing how to respond to it. The diagram on the next page illustrates these differences.

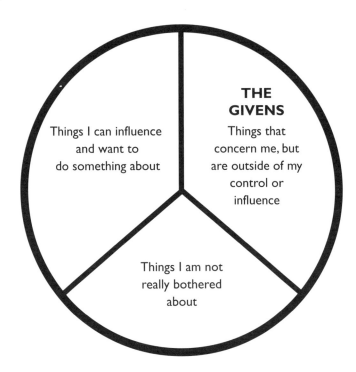

84. Coaching people you love

Emotions can get in the way of effectively coaching people you love or care for. Even if you can successfully separate yourself from the content of what the person is saying, that person might not appreciate your detached role. It helps to agree coaching ground rules and identify possible obstacles at the outset if you are coaching a partner. Even so, that person might not accept the help of someone so close to them. Likewise you might not be able to resist reacting to their responses, vocal tone or body language.

However, all is not lost if this is the case. A great relationship building exercise is to use your coaching skills to define joint umbrella goals, explore the strength of each other's reason why, generate possibilities, identify priorities, etc. You might want to consider a variety of short, medium and long-term differences you want to make in various aspects of your life.

"Love does not consist of gazing at each other,
but in looking outward together in the same direction."
Antoine de Saint-Exupery

With young children, you don't need to form coaching ground rules; you need to engage the imagination. (This is normally much easier to do with children than adults!) This can be great fun, as well as being beneficial, for them to develop high self-belief and work towards achieving worthwhile goals.

85. A few other uses for high quality questions

– written communication that invites people to think e.g. in preparation for meetings or project planning.

– during normal everyday conversations with friends and colleagues.

– in response to cynicism and negativity.

– during telephone conversations.

– as thought provokers.

– as agenda items in meetings.

– during performance reviews.

– to provoke discussion.

– to generate conversation.

– to assess the motivation and confidence of others.

– to produce ideas.

– to help anyone, including yourself, to think more clearly.

– to develop your manager.

86. Coaching upwards

By modifying your H.Q.Q.'s, and using the ThinkOn® Results Framework, you can successfully coach your manager to make a difference – often without that person even realising!

Imagine that your manager requests that you undertake a particular project and doesn't have the skills to gain your buy-in. Here are a few questions that could be adapted for use with your manager that would dramatically increase the probability of success:

– what specifically is the outcome you or others desire?

– how will we measure the success of the project?

– what is the timeframe?

– how achievable do you believe this to be within this timeframe?

– how important is this project in comparison to my other projects?

– how strong is your underlying reason for the completion of this project?

– what causes it to be strong?

– what ideas and possibilities have you already considered?

– what other possibilities would you like me to consider?

– who would you like me to involve?

– who else could possibly help?

– how can we gain their commitment to helping?

– what resources do you believe I will need?

– are you prepared to allow me to be accountable for making this happen?

Guiding your manager through a series of H.Q.Q.'s could result in a number of outcomes:

- you could gain lots of useful information that makes it easier to complete the project.

- your manager realises that the project is not as important as originally anticipated.

- your manager gains increased clarity about the way forward.

"Life is but an endless series of experiments."
Mahatma Gandhi

---

87. Answering a question with a question

Occasionally I get asked a question when I am coaching that indicates that the person is seeking to gain my approval or establish my confidence in their ability e.g. "Do you think I will succeed?"

- If I give an opinion, I would immediately become involved in the content. My typical responses might include:

- "It's not for me to judge, it's more important for you to answer the question."

- "Only you know the answer to that question. I believe you have the potential to succeed, what do you think?"

By asking this question, the individual might be indicating a need to increase their self-belief. Hence this needs to be explored by reflecting the question back.

**"Our deepest fear is not that we are inadequate.
Our deepest fear is that we are powerful beyond
measure. It is our light, not our darkness,
that most frightens us."**
Marianne Williamson

---

88. Listening skills

I have spent much of this book emphasising the need for high quality questioning skills. But, what about listening skills? They are important, but not as critical as the use of H.Q.Q.'s. I can coach a person to make a difference without listening to their answers to my structured H.Q.Q.'s, but I cannot coach a person purely by listening! However, good listening skills can enhance good coaching questions. Here are a few key points and tips:

- your thoughts can be a barrier, as effective listening requires energy and the ability to concentrate on the other person, rather than yourself.

- listen to the tone, pitch and speed of voice as well as the words that are spoken.

- listen for clues about confidence and self-belief levels. These can appear at any stage of the process and will be given in many guises.

- notice when you are not listening and become aware of the cause of your distraction.

- be honest and admit when you don't understand.

- check your understanding at regular intervals through the use of paraphrasing, reflecting feelings and summarising skills.

- use silence. You can't listen whilst you are talking.

"It has been said we have two ears and one mouth because we need to listen twice as much as we talk. That may be, but I also believe it's because it's twice as hard to listen!"
Mark Twain

- when paraphrasing, focus on the three or four key points the individual has made and repeat them back using similar words. Take care to just reiterate the facts stated without introducing new information or interpretations into your paraphrase.

End the paraphrase with a deliberate closed question to check your understanding. For example:

"So what's important is that X, Y and Z are completed before the project commences. Is that right?"

"Let me clarify my understanding from what you have said. Before you start the project, X, Y and Z need to be completed – is that a fair summary?"

By adding the closed question at the end of the paraphrase, it enables the individual to totally or partially agree/disagree. In reality, if you misunderstand, and inaccurately paraphrase, the individual is often unable to stop themselves from automatically correcting you. Hence the essential information is established, whether you are right or wrong in the accuracy of your paraphrase. Failure to ask the closed confirmation question means that an inaccurate assumption could easily be made.

**"When people talk, listen completely.
Most people never listen."
Ernest Hemingway**

Sometimes, when coaching, I pick up clues from vocal tone and body language that indicate the individual is experiencing an emotion that they are not verbally communicating. To establish what they are feeling, I use a technique called "reflecting feelings." This is where I reflect back to the person that I am picking up signals that they are feeling an emotion and not expressing it. For example:

"I get the impression that you feel frustrated about that. Am I right?"

"I'm getting vibes that you are not happy with the situation. Is that correct?"

Reflecting feelings differs from paraphrasing in several ways. With a paraphrase it is the expressed information (usually factual) that is clarified; with a reflection of feelings it is the unexpressed emotion that is clarified. A reflection of feelings does not focus on the content of what has been said – it is an interpretation of the various vocal tone and body language clues. Notice how in the previous examples I used a gentle introduction to the reflection of feeling. "I get the impression," is much less assumptive than, "I can tell how you are feeling." The deliberate closed question seeks to establish confirmation of understanding.

Using the reflecting feelings technique can build rapport and understanding at a deeper level than paraphrasing. It can be used to effectively check the strength of self-belief and reason why. For example:

"I get the impression that you are really not that bothered about achieving the goal. Is that right?"

Tip: when reflecting a feeling, describe the one emotion that you think the individual feels strongest.

Reflecting feelings is a subtle way for a coach to check their assumptions about an individual's self-confidence or feelings over a specified time period. For example:

"From what you've said, I sense that whilst you are not feeling confident about giving presentations now, you have been confident in the past about doing them. Is that true?"

There are four usual responses to a reflection of feelings:

1. Yes, that's right (confirmation)

2. No, I feel... (correction)

3. Yes and no (partial confirmation and correction)

4. Yes (but vocal tone indicates no)

The fourth of these responses requires challenging to establish the true feeling.

89. When coaching doesn't work

There are certain situations where coaching is either inappropriate or will not be productive. These include:

– when the individual does not want to make a difference, i.e. lack of reason why.

– when the individual does not want to be coached.

– when the individual immediately needs new knowledge or technical skills.

– when the individual lacks trust in the coach.

– when the individual requires counselling or therapy (in cases beyond your expertise, refer the individual to a specialist).

"By three methods we may learn wisdom:
first, by reflection which is noblest;
second, by imitation, which is the easiest;
and third, by experience, which is the bitterest."
Confucius

90. ThinkOn® as a 20 step self-coaching process

I was once asked to produce an outline of ThinkOn® as a linear process. The following twenty steps form a self-coaching process for your own use. Notice how familiar it is, now that you have understood the previous content of this book.

1. Define what you want and write a SMART goal in a single sentence.

2. Use your imagination to travel forward to the specific date of your goal and gather information (i.e. what you will see, hear and feel) that enables you to describe your goal in a detailed present tense.

3. Identify the reason why you want to make this difference.

4. Check the strength of your reason. (Strengthen motivation if necessary.)

5. Assess the level of your self-belief about achieving the goal. (Strengthen self-belief if necessary.)

6. Generate ideas by exploring the 10 possibility thinking areas, including:

   – tasks

   – resources

   – people to involve

   – implications

   – obstacles

   – ways of overcoming obstacles

7. Consider what help others can possibly be and how to gain their buy-in to your goal.

8. Continue to add to your possibilities.

9. Prioritise the most important ideas.

10. Convert these priorities into single sentence SMART sub-goals.

11. Repeat steps 5-9 for each sub-goal, if necessary.

12. Decide whom you will definitely involve and how to obtain their involvement.

13. Re-assess level of self-belief in achieving your goals.

14. Plan any personal development actions (if necessary.)

15. Check that your reason why is strong enough.

16. Plan your time by:

   – Blocking out time in your diary to work on each sub-goal.

   – Scheduling reviews to measure progress and results.

17. Take action.

18. Review progress and repeat steps 1-17 where appropriate.

19. Measure your results against your defined goal and sub-goals.

20. Celebrate success.

Remember, that whilst this might be a useful 20 step process to follow, it does not give the flexibility of applying ThinkOn® as a thinking system to enable you to move in different directions around the framework.

91. Practise, practise, practise

Here are a few final ideas to help you develop your coaching skills further:

– create opportunities to practise by offering to coach friends, family and work colleagues.

– recognise that it might be easier to get buy-in from some people by asking if they would like some "help with their thinking" – rather than offering to coach them.

– develop a co-coaching relationship with another person seeking to enhance their skills.

– ask for feedback from people you coach.

– find yourself a coach (select carefully and consider if you need someone who can also give you feedback).

– record a coaching session and ask for feedback.

– re-read this book.

– observe other great coaches.

– attend a coaching skills training programme.

– refer back to chapter 9 and assess yourself against my 30 beliefs of what makes a great ThinkOn® coach.

– ask yourself high quality questions about your own coaching ability and take responsibility for your continuing development.

– recognise and celebrate your success as a coach.

– practise, practise, practise.

92. Leave the how for later

The majority of people I meet and work with are too keen to get stuck into how to make a difference, without clearly specifying exactly what the difference is or why they want to make it. They then literally do get stuck and the difference does not get made.

> "Focus on the why and the what;
> leave the how for later."
> Andy Gilbert

When using ThinkOn® as a Solution Focused Thinking System to make a difference, it is essential to concentrate on the first two key principles, giving them sufficient time and attention before moving on.

You've read the book, so what difference are you going to make? I have included a few case studies and success stories in the final few pages of this book to give you an indication of how others have successfully applied ThinkOn® to help themselves, others and their organisation.

Decide what you want to do and why you want to do it. Leave the how for later. Then go make a difference and remember to celebrate your success. Ian and I would love to hear your success story of how you have made a difference for yourself or for someone else. It might even become a featured case study in the future – just a possibility!

> "Words are the most powerful drug used by mankind."
> Rudyard Kipling

SUCCESS STORIES, CASE STUDIES AND FURTHER INFORMATION

One of the most satisfying aspects of helping others to develop their ability to make a difference is celebrating success. We enjoy receiving the many letters, e-mails and photographs that are sent to us as evidence of people achieving their goals. To conclude this book, we have selected six examples to illustrate the diversity of application of the ThinkOn® system.

93. Mike's story – career success

An e-mail was received from Mike Currah earlier this year having applied the ThinkOn® system to changing his career. Here is his story.

"When attending a 3-day course, in October, I came to the conclusion that my current employer couldn't offer me the career development opportunities I wanted.

From the hotel I made contact with a previous boss, Brian (my 'best boss', for whom I had really enjoyed working) and asked him if he knew of any opportunities within his present company (principle five – Involve Others). He sounded enthusiastic and spoke very favourably about his company and I emailed him my C.V.

I wrote down the following SMART goal:

"By January 31st, to receive an offer letter for a brilliant job, to open it, smile and think 'Get In'."

I also began to apply seriously to job adverts, but initially with no positive responses – not getting first interviews for positions for which I thought I was well qualified.

Towards the end of November, there was a shock turn of events – it was announced that the factory which I was running was to be closed by the end of January! From a personal viewpoint, there was no guarantee that I would have a job and could be facing redundancy.

This event really focused my mind on getting a new position (I certainly now had a strong Reason Why – principle one). I revamped my cover letter to not mention 'textiles' as I felt the stigma attached to the industry was stopping me getting first interviews. I used the 'Me plc' framework to think about my unique selling points when competing with other candidates.

First and second interviews started to come through, possibly from the sub-conscious effect of having a much stronger reason why than previously. However, although I got through to the last three for two jobs, I couldn't get to the offer stage. The date was now 26th January and I was beginning to wonder whether I would achieve my SMART goal!

Then, out of the blue, I got a phone call on Friday afternoon from Brian, the previous boss whom I had contacted first. I had visited the business in December, then had a couple of meetings cancelled and assumed things had gone cold. He offered me a really exciting position, as a Product Transfer Leader within the computer systems manufacturing division. This was a move away from a site-based role, with far more variety, which were job elements which I was certainly looking for.

The HR Director rang me on Monday 29th January, and said an offer letter and contract would be put in the post and should arrive on the 30th. At this point I was absolutely certain that it wouldn't – it was going to arrive on the 31st to match my goal.

Tuesday came and went. On the 31st, with my stomach churning, I got a call from home to say that an official looking letter had arrived. I went home early to open it and the rest is history.

I start on March 2nd."

94. Anna's story – business success

Anna Clancy is an Accredited ThinkOn® Coach with Royal & SunAlliance. In achieving her accreditation, Anna submitted evidence that she had made a measurable business difference through coaching others.

One of the people she coached described her as, "not a normal person – she is so enthusiastic and encouraging, and great at getting people involved." Another commented how Anna helped her to define a goal, and increase her self-belief from a 7 to a 10, at which point she knew she could achieve her goal. Anna then coached her to look at the possibilities of how she could achieve this, before prioritising and putting a plan in place. "I then took personal responsibility and took the appropriate action and achieved my goal."

One of the measurable differences that resulted from Anna's coaching was a time saving of 56 hours per month for a credit control team. Time that is now being better spent on the collection of overdue debt from brokers.

95. Tracey's story – sporting success

Tracey Lovell is also an Accredited ThinkOn® Coach. As well as coaching others to make a difference in the workplace, Tracey has also applied ThinkOn® to attain sporting success. Here is her story.

"Gardiners netball team started their new season in September. Our previous season had not been a great success so we were determined to do something to make a difference this year.

We did some planning and had arranged for a new coach to help us with training sessions. As games went by, there was a slight improvement, however there was still something missing. What was it?

In December, I was invited to attend a 4-day course ran by Andy Gilbert, who would teach us the art of solution focused coaching.

At the end of the week I was feeling truly inspired. As an activist I was naturally eager to experiment using the system and test if I could make it work before coaching my colleagues.

Having learnt about the seven principles I now knew what was missing. We already had a strong reason why (principle one) and we knew what our defined goal (principle two) was:

"By 30ᵗʰ April next year Gardiners Netball Club will be promoted to Division 2."

We had generated possibilities and identified priorities and used the 3 P's and also involved others (principle five) by appointing a coach.

What we needed was a huge dose of self-belief (principle four). I knew unless we worked on this we would not succeed. We started to work on this for the remaining part of the season. We were learning tactics, however we just didn't believe we could do it.

I got the team together and told them all about how important it is to believe in ourselves. I gave some examples from Andy's book and they were interested in giving it a try. As we know, there isn't any such word as try. This was time to get us into positive mode.

We started by concentrating on our positive self-talks and using affirmation statements effectively. We all took personal responsibility (principle six) for giving ourselves a self-talk on the way to netball and using affirmation statements.

For example, as Goal Shooter of the team I would say, "I am a good goal shooter and I score lots of goals". I would say this repeatedly on my journey to each game and the others would do similar.

We also worked on visualisation. We talked about the presentation night when we would receive our medals. How would we feel? What would people say? What would they look like? How would we celebrate our success?

Finally, we already had our defined goal (principle two) however, we needed sub-goals to keep us going.

We decided to set ourselves a goal at the start of each quarter. For example, "By 1.15pm on 16th December we will have scored 15 goals." This lifted our team spirit and it became more fun and more focused.

We have measured the results (principle seven). We have reached the end the season and on 11th May Gardiners Netball Club will be celebrating their success by picking up our promotion medals.

Our visualisation will become a realisation.

Thank you, Andy, for introducing me to a system that works in practice and really is fun to use."

96. Natalie's story – child success

Natalie Johnston, another ThinkOn® Accredited Coach, sent me a lengthy list of short success stories. One in particular caught my eye:

"My friend's 8 year old daughter with long division!... most nights were fights over homework and "I can't do it."

I just passed the The Art of Making A Difference book on to my friend, and to increase her daughter's self-belief, they incorporated "I can do" phrases to sing whilst she was skipping.

Three nights later – gold star in her jotter!!"

97. Kraft Foods – financial success

ThinkOn® started working with Kraft Foods, USA in 2011. This started at the Champaign Illinois plant which is Kraft Foods' largest manufacturing facility worldwide. Its production focuses on processed cheese, macaroni and cheese dinners, salad dressings, miracle whip and mayonnaise. The facility sits on 89 acres of property, houses 39 production lines, a large warehouse and employs over 1200 people.

Our work supported the delivery of their 'All in to Win' strategy, the purpose of which was to drive change to gain greater collaboration between different areas of the facility in order to achieve the performance increases required by the organisation. The plant was already performing at world class level so a breakthrough in thinking was required in order to get the transformational shift in results they required.

Our approach:

- Development of the Leadership and Continuous Improvement Teams in Results Focused Thinking techniques. This involved the introduction to the ThinkOn® Results Framework and coaching toolkit. Outcomes included: more engaging leadership styles, increased levels of innovation, faster achievement of results, time saved and a much greater belief in their ability to deliver the results.

- Cascade of this approach vertically throughout the organisation including shift and production line operators. This resulted in 'them' and 'us' barriers being broken down, people at all levels of the business becoming aligned to common goals and making tangible, measurable differences to their targets.

- Engagement events for larger groups to help them embrace change and buy into the difference being made.

- One-to-one coaching with key members of the Leadership Team plus Senior Team development workshops leading to greater unity and cohesion.

- Practical Change Management workshops for key change work streams enabling them to link tools and techniques in real time to real initiatives.

- A series of 90-day challenges in place for individuals and teams to take personal responsibility for initiating change and making measurable differences.

Christine Bense, Plant Manager, submitted her project diary entries to us on a regular basis and here are some extracts over the course of a year:

February 1st

"Hosted our first of five ideation sessions today – engaged 40 people from across the business in a structured event using possibility thinking tools to identify $7M of potential new savings ideas. Not bad for one day."

March 16th

"One of my department managers found an 'outlier' idea off one of our possibility thinking sheets. It didn't make the short list originally but with further investigation, looks to be worth over $300K to us and is likely scalable across the US processed cheese network."

April 17th

"Reviewed the results of our Q1 90-Day Challenge today…25 people delivered over $5M in full year savings, claiming the Challenge changed their thinking, improved collaboration, drove accountability and had a notable impact on the results they achieved. We're ahead of plan three months in."

April 27th

"600 people participated in possibility thinking over the last week as part of our 7-day challenge. The result? $800K of full year savings. Another good example of 'All in to Win'!"

June 22nd

"We reviewed the results of our Q2 60-day challenges this morning and learned that 32 of us delivered almost £5M in full year savings! That tops our Q1 challenge results (considering we had 30 less days)!"

September 14th

"We reviewed our Q3 90-day Challenge and learned that between 61 people, we delivered a whopping $8.5M in full year savings, identified $1M in new ideas for the next year and made several improvements to key work processes. The best part was seeing everyone sharing their successes with each other, particularly those who weren't sure THEY could make a difference and seeing the pride in peoples' faces. We are living proof that thinking differently leads to different behaviours and a different level of results."

December 14th

"Today we reviewed the results of our Q4 90-day challenge and once again, I was impressed with the outcome! Collectively, participants delivered about $5M in full year benefit to the business (a combination of cost savings and inventory reduction). What was most pleasing to see was the level of collaboration within teams and hearing people describe how the challenge focused them to achieve things they wouldn't have otherwise."

January 10th

"Another ThinkOn® event has come and gone. We trained a fresh batch of 16 employees and kicked off our Q1 90-day challenge with well over 100 participants – that's 4 times as many people as we had this time last year."

98. John's poem – personal success

This poem about self-belief was written by John Statham, a participant on a ThinkOn® coaching programme. It made me and the rest of the participants smile. I hope it does the same for you!

A Poem About Myself

Now that I've reached the age of fifty,
My brain becomes a lot less nifty,
Arteries begin to harden,
Spend more time out in the garden,
See my waistline start to spread,
See more skin atop my head,
Reach out for my pipe and slippers,
Soon my kids will have their nippers,
Wonder where the years all went,
Spend the evenings somnolent.
But – bugger that for a game of soldiers,
Stop the moans about getting older.
"Too old," is all inside your head.
Get on with it, ThinkOn instead!"

John Statham

99. Applying the ThinkOn® System at four levels

From reading this book it is easy to think that ThinkOn® is all about coaching, but remember ThinkOn® was not developed as a coaching model (refer to chapter 6 about the original research). Its broadest application is as a thinking system which provides both structure and flexibility in the following areas:

The following chapter provides a brief insight into the broadest application of helping organisations develop a solution focused thinking culture.

100. Leadership thinking and cultural transformation

Imagine if everyone who worked in an organisation shared the same thinking system, with an easy to understand language, aligned to clearly defined business goals. It makes sense! If everyone is equipped to use the same IT system, why not equip people to use the same shared thinking system?

In addition to my research and writing activities, much of my time is spent working with leaders in organisations developing business improvement and leadership thinking programmes to enable business results to be achieved quicker and more cost effectively. As you might expect, achieving large-scale change can often be quite complex.

> "The old guard in any society resents new methods, for old guards wear the decorations and medals won by waging battle in the old accepted manner."
> Martin Luther King, Jr

From 2000 onwards, the ThinkOn® team have developed and tested ways of embedding ThinkOn® as a thinking system using a rigorous installation methodology to guarantee measurable results. The ThinkOn® system, which you have become familiar with in this book, has been developed into the ThinkOn® Leadership Framework to analyse and facilitate change at a macro level.

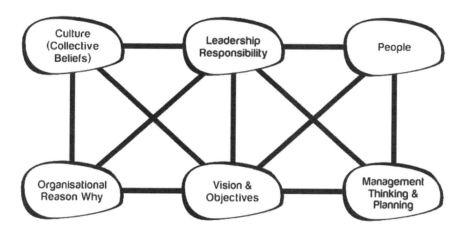

ThinkOn® Leadership Framework

So, instead of Personal Responsibility this becomes Leadership Responsibility; the People involved include employees, customers and other stakeholders; the goal becomes the Vision; the individual Self-Belief becomes the Culture of the organisation; the Reason Why becomes an Organisational Reason Why (e.g. shareholder value); and Possibilities & Priorities becomes a Management Thinking activity in line with the business objectives and direction given by the leadership team.

Adopting a systems thinking approach to organisational change means that we need to consider the individual elements and their impact upon each other. Potentially there will be a need to take action and measure the results of each element. A different set of questions can now be asked to analyse the macro differences leaders are seeking to make and identify weaknesses in the system.

- What is the organisational reason for seeking change?

- What is the leadership vision?

- How strong is the existing culture to support the vision?

- How is the vision being communicated to managers responsible for the planning and implementation?

- How effectively are the objectives being communicated to other people (employees, customers, suppliers, etc.) to obtain their commitment?

Now I realise that this might all seem a bit much if you only want to apply ThinkOn® at a personal effectiveness level. However, there might be a time when your reason why is sufficiently strong to help others, and possibly an organisation, make a greater difference. If that time is now, I recommend you read a couple of my other books, "How to Make A Difference by Transforming Managers into Leaders" and "How to Save Time and Money by Managing Organisational Change Effectively".

> "Your legacy should be that you made it better
> than it was when you got it."
> Lee Iacocca

101. ThinkOn® information and resources

You can discover more about our full range of products, training programmes, online learning, coaching resources and mobile coaching applications by visiting our company website at www.gomadthinking.com or call us for a chat on +44 (0) 1509 891313.

If you liked the practical style of this book, and are interested in reading further publications written by myself and the team, you might want to consider the following:

How to Make A Difference by Transforming Managers into Leaders
(Practical tips and ideas to develop your leadership ability.)

How to Save Time and Money by Managing Organisational Change Effectively
(A practical guide to help managers handle people's reaction to organisational change.)

The Art of Making A Difference
(A powerful guide for achieving personal and business success and a great introduction to Solution Focused Thinking.)

How to Save Time and Money by Managing Meetings Effectively
(A practical guide to help make a difference by effectively preparing for and facilitating meetings to achieve greater results.)

Engage and Empower
(277 practical ways to improve productivity.)

If you are seeking to make a difference within an organisation and would like to have a discussion about any aspect of applying ThinkOn® as a catalyst for change management, innovation, cultural transformation, leadership, business improvement or management development then please contact one of the ThinkOn® team.

Go M.A.D. Thinking
Pocket Gate Farm
Off Breakback Road
Woodhouse Eaves
Leicestershire
LE12 8RS United Kingdom
t: +44 (0) 1509 891313
e: info@gomadthinking.com
w: www.gomadthinking.com

NOTES

NOTES

NOTES

NOTES